HONORÉ DE BALZAC

My Reading

PETER BROOKS

HONORÉ DE BALZAC

OXFORD
UNIVERSITY PRESS

OXFORD

UNIVERSITY PRESS

Great Clarendon Street, Oxford, OX2 6DP,
United Kingdom

Oxford University Press is a department of the University of Oxford.
It furthers the University's objective of excellence in research, scholarship,
and education by publishing worldwide. Oxford is a registered trade mark of
Oxford University Press in the UK and in certain other countries

First Edition published in 2022

Impression: 1

Published in the United States of America by Oxford University Press
198 Madison Avenue, New York, NY 10016, United States of America

British Library Cataloguing in Publication Data
Data available

Library of Congress Control Number: 2022932396

ISBN 978–0–19–284670–9

DOI: 10.1093/oso/9780192846709.001.0001

Printed and bound in the UK by
Clays Ltd, Elcograf S.p.A.

SERIES INTRODUCTION

This series is built on a simple presupposition: that it helps to have a book recommended and discussed by someone who cares for it. Books are not purely self-sufficient: they need people and they need to get to what is personal within them.

The people we have been seeking as contributors to *My Reading* are readers who are also writers: novelists and poets; literary critics, outside as well as inside universities, but also thinkers from other disciplines—philosophy, psychology, science, theology, and sociology—beside the literary; and, not least of all, intense readers whose first profession is not writing itself but, for example, medicine, or law, or a non-verbal form of art. Of all of them we have asked: what books or authors feel as though they are deeply *yours*, influencing or challenging your life and work, most deserving of rescue and attention, or demanding of feeling and use?

What is it like to love this book? What is it like to have a thought or idea or doubt or memory, not cold and in abstract, but live in the very act of reading? What is it like to feel, long after, that this writer is a vital part of your life? We ask our authors to respond to such bold questions by writing not conventionally but personally—whatever "personal" might mean, whatever form or style it might take, for them as individuals. This does not mean overt confession at the expense of a chosen book or author; but nor should our writers be afraid of making autobiographical connections. What was wanted was whatever made for their own hardest thinking in careful relation to quoted sources and specifics. The work was to go on in the taut and resonant space between these readers and their chosen books. And the interest within that area begins precisely when it is no longer clear how much is coming from the text, and how much is coming from its readers—where that distinction is no longer easily tenable because neither is sacrificed to the other. That would show what reading meant at its most serious and how it might have relation to an individual life.

Out of what we hope will be an ongoing variety of books and readers, *My Reading* offers personal models of what it is like to care about particular authors, to recreate through specific examples imaginative versions of what those authors and works represent, and to show their effect upon a reader's own thinking and development.

ANNE CHENG
PHILIP DAVIS
JACQUELINE NORTON
MARINA WARNER
MICHAEL WOOD

CONTENTS

1. Balzac: Reading for More   1

2. Fangs and Kisses   25

3. Writing, Talking, Devouring Presses   50

4. The Shape of Time   75

5. To Say Everything   102

Acknowledgments   137
Further Reading   138
Notes   140
Index   145

1

BALZAC: READING
FOR MORE

Pre-Balzac

I began, as an adolescent, with Bach and the baroque, slipping slowly forward toward the classical: Mozart and Beethoven; Berlioz and the Romantics only came later. In reading it was somewhat the same. Stendhal became, when I was in my twenties, the favorite. I wrote about him and what I took to be the line of his predecessors in the eighteenth century, especially Choderlos de Laclos, author of *Les Liaisons dangereuses*: a literature of wit and social intelligence, intent upon understanding human beings in their social settings, a line reaching back to La Rochefoucauld and Madame de Lafayette. Survival in society demanded attention, intelligence, an analytic understanding of others: "Machiavellian intelligence," as contemporary students of neuroscience describe the workings of our minds, but also the lessons of Castiglione, who in *The Courtier* teaches us to make ourselves agreeable to others, to fashion our appearance and manners to what makes us effective in society. What is needed in this literature of worldliness is well represented in the title of a treatise by Torquato Accetto, *Della dissimulazione onesta*: that kind of fashioning of the self that is "honest," that is to say, right and decent for you to play a role in the social milieu. As mention of *Les Liaisons dangereuses* implies, sexual interaction becomes in this world a kind of test of who you are when façades are stripped away, maybe the ultimate form of social intercourse.[1]

Stendhal, whose grandfather raised him in admiration of Voltaire and other masters of eighteenth-century free thought and worldly manners, belongs to this tradition while admiring the newfound freedom of the post-Revolutionary age, and the tenderness made possible by Rousseau and the early Romantics he discovered in Italy. Stendhal was just right for me: he seemed to contemplate his novelistic world from a certain height, indulging his young heroes in their inept attempts at amorous conquest, for instance, with imperturbable urbanity. He was accustomed to the world's rogueries, never unduly shocked by them, yet always clear that did not subscribe to them. And while he stood superior to the gropings and mistakes of Julien Sorel, Lucien Leuwen, and Fabrice del Dongo, it was evident also that he admired their spirit, admired them most of all when they broke with social convention and the expected—when they said or did something wildly unexpected even when it shattered their careers, or took them to the guillotine. The ever-renewed dialogue of Stendhal with his characters was to me—and is still—a source of immense pleasure. I felt part of an entertaining conversation that I could never have anywhere else, one carried forward at the highest level of both analytic intelligence and good fellowship. He made me feel intelligent.

I reread Stendhal always with pleasure; most recently I reread most of the unfinished *Lucien Leuwen,* in its second half an astonishingly contemporary novel of politics, power, and the disturbing choices they pose to the individual in society. I almost decided to write this account of "my reading" on Stendhal, and certainly I could. Yet something else beckoned. To return to my musical loves: I moved on, not to love Bach any less but to encompass Brahms, Verdi, and Wagner, for instance. The love of opera, closed to me as an adolescent, wasn't predictable from my early tastes. My evolution has been toward a greater tolerance for the stagey and melodramatic, and also for the anarchic. I note that in politics I have constantly moved left, so that I now believe in the radical upheaval of institutions I once accepted. I love Stendhal still, but I feel called upon to engage someone I perhaps love less but feel to be absolutely crucial to understanding modernity, the way we live now, and the way we read now. And that is Balzac.

Finding Balzac

When as a young teacher my very conservatively managed academic department decided to entrust me with a seminar on a subject of my own choosing, it wasn't Stendhal that I picked. I chose to teach the seminar on Balzac, though I by no means mastered the novelist and his work. I had a somewhat inchoate idea of who he was and what he meant and how you went about making a selection from his ninety novels and tales. But I think that was really the point: Balzac and *The Human Comedy* seemed like largely uncharted territory waiting to be explored, mapped, made into something that we in the seminar could understand and make our own. Not that there weren't plenty of expositors of Balzac before us. Especially, there was Henry James. Anglo-American criticism had never come to terms with the fact that this most refined of novelists, who dealt in the stuff of consciousness, admired the rambunctious and melodramatic Balzac above all other precursors. When James returned after years of exile to the United States in 1904–1905, just as *The Golden Bowl* was coming out, he toured the country from north to south and from coast to coast delivering a lecture entitled "The Lesson of Balzac." Strange to think that he believed his compatriots needed that particular lesson. But for James, Balzac represented a novelistic tradition that was enormously important, that he thought it urgent to share on his native soil, which he insisted upon finding culturally somewhat barren. From Philadelphia to Saint Louis and Indianapolis and San Francisco, he lectured on Balzac, claiming in his attention to this novelist of social density to bootstrap the American novel.

Balzac from early on seemed a challenge to me, as I think he was to James. How do you come to terms with this immense production, often of uneven quality, often in its greatest moments perilously over-the-top? I present no theories here, only an experience of reading. Why, once you begin, is Balzac addictive? Why does he make you want more? And how indeed is that demand for more built into the very substance of his fiction? What are the kinds of questions he elicits from the reader? How does he convince us that his subject, largely France of the 1820s, 30s, and 40s, bears on our understanding not only of that society but of our own as well? Oscar Wilde famously said the nineteenth century as we know it was invented by Balzac.[2] The typical Wildean paradox—the precedence of art over life—rings very true in this case. We know the historical period Balzac writes about by way of his writings: its characters, forces, dynamic energy, its brutal selection of winners and losers, perhaps most of all its promotion of the cash nexus, with the consequent eclipse of older systems of social selection, that has come to dominate all else. Balzac invented the nineteenth century by making it visible and legible. Historians still today find his work a source of insight about post-Revolutionary, post-Napoleonic France caught up in the dynamics of the new and seeking to understand the new rules of the game. Balzac sees and he expounds the beginnings of modernity.

I began, probably like most other readers of Balzac, with his novel that has most attained the status of classic, *Père Goriot (Le Père Goriot)*. Initial confusion: why is the novel titled for the sad old exploited father of the two daughters who thanks to the money he has made—not very honorably: in cornering the grain market during the great famine of the French Revolution—have married, one into the aristocracy, the other to an unscrupulous banker? Eventually we will understand that the novel profoundly is about the collapse of paternal authority. Père Goriot is the butt of jokes in the Pension Vauquer, the greasy boarding house where he lives, along with the young protagonist Eugène de Rastignac, from an aristocratic but penniless provincial family that has sent him to Paris to study law. There is a lot of presentation going on at the start of the novel: description of place (what weighs down so many nineteenth-century novels, from Walter Scott onwards), introductions of people, exposition of situations. Yet as your eyes start to glaze over you realize something else is happening in the prose you are reading. The furniture starts to come menacingly alive: you encounter "those indestructible pieces of furniture, banished everywhere else, but placed here like the debris of civilization in the Hospice for the Incurable."[3] Description insists, reaching a kind of crescendo: "To explain how much this furniture is old, knocked up, rotted, trembling, worm-eaten, one-armed, one-eyed, invalid, moribund, would require a description that would slow down too much the interest of this story…" The narrator doesn't cease to describe, but description has become manic. For the residents of the Pension as well: "These lodgers made one sense dramas past or ongoing; not those dramas played out under the footlights, between painted scenery, but mute, living dramas, icy dramas that tore hotly at the heart, dramas long drawn out" (P 3:57/S 13–14). And then, zeroing in on one of the boarders, Mlle Michonneau: "What acid had stripped this creature of her feminine forms? She must have been pretty and well made: was it vice, sorrow, cupidity? Had she loved too much, had she been a go-between or merely a harlot?…"

It maybe depends on your mood: you might find this too much, an overspiced dish where you would prefer something cool and subtle, more like Stendhal in fact. What is the appeal of Balzac's summons here? What kind of reading does he invite us to, demand of us, really? This becomes clearer when we encounter Eugène de Rastignac, who has returned to Paris from summer vacation, and returned also from his first soirée at the grand house of his distant cousin, Vicomtesse Claire de Beauséant, who sits at the very summit of the Faubourg Saint-Germain aristocracy—the old titled families that in this period of the Restoration, following Revolution and Napoleon's hectic reign, set the tone for society. Rastignac is smitten with "the visible delights of material Paris," and with the instinctive understanding that the way forward and up lies with the glorious women he has met at Madame de Beauséant's.

> To be young, to have a thirst for society, to have hunger for a woman and to see two houses open their doors to you! To have a foot in the Faubourg Saint-Germain at the Vicomtesse de Beauseant's, a knee in the Chausée d'Antin at the Comtesse de Restaud's! To gaze into the vista of the salons of Paris lined up before you, and to think you are good looking enough to find aid and protection in a woman's

heart! To feel yourself ambitious enough to give a proud kick to the tightrope you must walk with the assurance of the acrobat who won't fall, and to have found in a charming woman the best of balancing poles!   (P 3: 77–8/S 38)

This is what Balzacian ambition is like. It's naked and unabashed. It works through women, who in their Parisian manifestation are objects of both sexual and social desire: sex points the way to social success. It triggers a dangerous high wire act that will work for Rastignac but precipitate some other young men (such as Lucien in *Lost Illusions*) to ruin. Above all it is a thirst and a hunger: a need to ingest the world, to devour it. If orality is the first stage of our need as infants, a need for the breast as nourishment but then as a kind of hallucinated object that can never wholly fulfill the imaginary demands it creates, Balzac's young heroes are its most naked protagonists. Their needs are undisguised. They must have it all, the nourishment needed and what lies beyond need, the satisfactions of unlimited desire.

This is what, I now think, drove my early readings of *Père Goriot*—drove them through an inadequate French vocabulary and a confused sense of who was what and where in the Paris social landscape. Jacques Lacan, if I understand him correctly, says that desire is born from the split between need and demand. Need is satisfied by nourishment. Demand is something else: it is demand for recognition, and always absolute. Desire then seeks to satisfy needs—nourishment, sexual and social fulfillment—but those are never quite enough; they don't satisfy the absolute imperatives left over from demand. Desire is driven forward in Faustian manner, seeking always more, always some additional satisfaction. It knows no rest. Nor does Rastignac, nor his reader. The figure of Balzacian ambition is also the figure of the kind of reading he asks for, insists on. It is reading as hunger and thirst. Much later in the novel, Rastignac will describe with some lucidity the relationship he has established with Delphine de Nucingen, the Goriot daughter who is married to the banker Nucingen but not at all satisfied by him. It's when Rastignac realizes Delphine will insist upon going to Madame de Beauséant's grand farewell ball despite the fact that her abandoned father is in his death agony: "Whether she were infamous or sublime, he adored this woman for the sensual pleasures he had brought her as dowry, and for those he had received in turn; just as Delphine loved Rastignac as much as Tantalus would have loved the angel who would have satisfied his hunger, or quenched the thirst of his parched throat." (P 3:263/S 253). How to unpack this? "Love" here is figured as Delphine's sexual awakening, after years of marriage, by the fierce desire that Rastignac brings her as "dowry," which in turn brings him gratification. And figured as the satisfaction of hunger and thirst brought to someone for whom satisfaction seemed out of reach. That's what sex is like, that's where ambition brings you.

Delphine is the right object of desire for Rastignac because love for her can be converted into money. In fact the first kiss he receives from her results from his success at gambling with money she provides him: his beginner's luck brings her 7,000 francs with which to pay off debts incurred by her former lover Henri de Marsay. (Don't let yourself get into thinking de Marsay a mere cad, even though he is: he'll end up prime minister of France.) If sex can satisfy desire, up to a point, money alone can assuage need. Vautrin, the ostensible businessman who dwells in the Pension Vauquer, another possible father-figure who will eventually stand revealed as an escaped convict and criminal mastermind, provides Rastignac with a cool analysis of his situation: "Do you know what you need, at the rate you are going on? A million, without delay." (P 3:136/S 108) And Vautrin lays out the alternatives. If Rastignac thinks he can get ahead through the practice of law, he'll end up among twenty thousand others, some of whom would sell out their families to advance an inch, all like spiders in a jar fighting for air. Vautrin proposes instead to provide an immediate solution: he will arrange a duel in which a friend of his who is an expert swordsman will kill young Michel-Frédéric Taillefer, whose sister Victorine lives in poverty in the Pension Vauquer because her father believes her illegitimate. Her brother dead, she'll become her father's only heir, acceding to an immense fortune (which Jean-Frédéric Taillefer gained by murdering a German businessman and arranging things so that his best friend takes the rap and is executed for the crime). Rastignac has to refuse: Vautrin has laid bare the stakes too starkly. But the goal remains. It may take a bit longer to reach, through Delphine rather than Victorine, but the crime committed will be less glaring.

But wait. My revelation of the criminal origin of Taillefer's fortune isn't fully given in *Père Goriot*. It comes from a novella called *The Red Inn* (*L'Auberge rouge*). Its publication predates *Père Goriot*, though its principal characters bore other names at that point. It seems that Balzac in writing *Père Goriot* refers to the criminal past of this character—who doesn't really come on stage, but is known through the killing of his son and his reinstatement of Victorine as his daughter—which he then fills in only later, in his rewrite of *The Red Inn* as the story of old Taillefer, and the fate of Victorine, possibly again rejected as a love object because her potential suitor learns of the sordid origins of her money. Our reading of *Père Goriot*, urged forward by the desiring young hero, opens up a kind of sideways possibility, as with a moment of hypertext. We no doubt want to pursue Rastignac's career to its end, but we have also been offered the possibility of adding something to it.

More

It was while engaged in writing *Père Goriot* that Balzac exclaimed to his beloved sister Laure that he was in the process of becoming a genius. He had at first named his hero Eugène de Massiac. Then he crossed out Massiac on his manuscript and substituted Rastignac. Eugène de Rastignac existed already, in the novel published a few years earlier called *The Fatal Skin* (*La Peau de chagrin*), where he is a somewhat older cynical and amiable fellow who takes the young hero of that novel under his protection. What did it mean to baptize his twenty-year-old hero with the name of someone he'd already staged at age thirty-two? It's not quite that he was writing a prequel to *The Fatal Skin*, where Rastignac is not a fully developed character. It represents instead some new understanding of fictional economy. There was something to be gained from presenting a character who had a prior existence, if only in minor fashion and at a later point in his life. He carried with him a certain weight and bulk from his prior appearance. As we read on in *Père Goriot*, we discover—maybe on our own, maybe from footnotes or an introduction—that many of the other characters appear in other novels as well. Madame de Beauséant was already the sad heroine of *The Abandoned Woman* (*La femme abandonnée*), which recounts her retreat from society after her desertion by her lover and her grand farewell ball, which we witness in *Père Goriot*. Delphine de Nucingen will appear in many other novels, and her banker husband, the Baron de Nucingen, will give the impression of near ubiquity, since the banker is a crucial player in this emerging capitalist society (he also will enrich his wife's lover, Rastignac) and her sister Anastasie de Restaud will be of importance in particular in *Gobseck*, the novella devoted to the moneylender who appears in *Père Goriot* and dozens of other novels. And Vautrin, arrested and returned to prison in *Père Goriot*, will make a spectacular return toward the end of *Lost Illusions (Illusions perdues)* disguised as a Spanish priest and then utterly dominate its sequel, *A Harlot High and Low (Splendeurs et misères des courtisanes)*. Even the swordsman whom Vautrin engages to kill young Taillefer, Colonel Franchessini, pops up again.

Is this maybe becoming vertiginous, a crowd of characters whose lives extend beyond the limits of this one novel? You can of course read *Père Goriot* without paying any attention to the various other incarnations of its characters, in ignorance of what's become known as the *retour des personnages*, the return of the same fictional beings. And that's fine, the novel stands on its own. But if you get caught up in following the fate of one or more of the characters elsewhere, you find yourself in a new mode of reading that Balzac invented. It's not the orderly succession of story-prequel-sequel that we have become more used to in the cyclic novels of Emile Zola or John Galsworthy and in the successful television serial that renews over the years by moving forward in the characters' lives and sometimes also back. Balzac defended his somewhat messy presentation of his characters in non-chronological order, often caught in their later lives before we learn of their earlier ones, by saying that life is a "mosaic."[4] We don't know people in the orderly manner of *Who's Who*. They come to us in fragments.

Balzac invents a new form of reading because once we have strayed beyond the single novel—when, say, we add to *Père Goriot* the novella *Gobseck,* which sheds a very different light on the climactic scenes of the former when it enters into the drama of the Restaud family, the Comte de Restaud's attempt to save the family fortune from Anastasie's wild expenditures, her attempt to protect her two illegitimate children from disinheritance—we enter upon another kind of reading experience that we may find confusing but mostly exhilarating. These characters take on a new heft. The changed lighting from one text to the other forces us into a kind of stereoscopic vision that makes them stand out in greater relief, and makes facile judgments on their behavior seem irrelevant. If we then move on, say, to *The House of Nucingen (La Maison Nucingen)*—a startlingly modern, nearly cubist kind of a narrative, showing the same person from different angles—we learn all about how Rastignac made his fortune as well as the trail of tears left by Nucingen's financial shenanigans. This is important. When at the end of *A Harlot High and Low* (if we push that far) Vautrin, now unmasked and returned to his "true" name, Jacques Collin, announces that he is renouncing crime in order to join the police and serve as an instrument of "order and repression," he notes that his acts as an outlaw were simply the mirror image of those Nucingen got away with legally. Outlaw and cop are essentially the same in a society which has lost all true principles of organization.

Reading from one novel to another in this manner mimes Rastignac's desire to devour the world, to ingest it—true not only for him but also so many other young men who hope to make it in the big city, Lucien de Rubempré and Victurnien d'Esgrignon and Raphaël de Valentin, and even a woman such as the aspiring writer Dinah de la Baudraye. There has to be always more. Once you have started you can't stop. Reading becomes devourment and what we now call bingeing: not stopping at one, not pacing out episodes but moving pell-mell through them. In Balzac, it doesn't matter in what order you do it. Life, as he said, is mosaic, and you can pick up the tesserae in any order, no order. Ideally, as the French experimental novelist Michel Butor who was a great Balzacian put it, *The Human Comedy* is one novel, and ideally you should read it all. That doesn't mean you are going to or must. It's rather that you know that there is ever more awaiting you if your appetite doesn't flag. There is another course in the kitchen, if you are up to it. The fictional world extends endlessly before you.

And this world is crowded with acquaintances, people you've met before or perceived off in corners at large gatherings or heard about in the mouths of others. Diane, originally Duchesse de Maufrigneuse then Princesse de Cadignan, audaciously places on her coffee table the album in which she has preserved portraits of perhaps thirty former lovers; we know them all, we have a dizzying sense of old friends recalled to us as she embarks upon her final and only true love, Daniel d'Arthez, the renowned novelist whom we first met as a poor aspiring writer who befriends Lucien de Rubempré in *Lost Illusions*. When Félix de Vandenesse in *A Daughter of Eve (Une fille d'Eve)* appears as a composed and somewhat cold married man trying to break up the nascent affair between his wife and the writer Raoul Nathan, we remember Nathan, now a facile playwright, as someone who seemed a major novelistic talent to the young Lucien in *Lost Illusions*, and we remember Félix himself as the frustrated young suitor of Henriette de Mortsauf in *The Lily of the Valley (Le Lys dans la vallée)*, a fearsome story that may in some manner explain his seemingly diminished eros. But it's up to us to make that inference—the novel demonstrates what Félix is now like but does not insist on an explanation. And when you have a gathering of well-known characters, for instance at the after-party following a big reception given by the novelist Félicité des Touches (who publishes under the pen name Camille Maupin), you can feel you are yourself a comfortable member of the gathering. Here's Delphine de Nucingen again, and Henri de Marsay, once her lover and now a powerful political figure, and the Baron de Nucingen, and the doctor, Horace Bianchon, who shared Rastignac's humble origins in the Pension Vauquer, and the journalist Emile Blondet we know from *Lost Illusions*, and General de Montriveau who co-stars in *La Duchesse de Langeais*.

I don't find it easy to describe the effect of these returning characters as you read from novel to novel. It's partly delight at meeting someone you already know, and already know so much about. You could I suppose be told about Félix de Vandenesse's youthful love for Henriette de Mortsauf in a flashback in *A Daughter of Eve*, but I don't think it would have the same effect as having known him in an entirely different context, at a different point in his life. In observing him as he maneuvers to bring his wife, Marie-Angélique de Granville, back into the marriage bond, we sense that his prior experience of frustrated love with Henriette, and the kind of vengeance she metes out after her death, in the testamentary letter that makes him feel castrated, and then the added vengeance of his new love interest, Natalie de Manerville—who tells him she's not going to compete with the ghost of a beloved he carries within him—has made him wise in the ways of love but also robbed him of his former capacity for passion. There is an unspoken depth to the character that comes from elsewhere, from what we've already read of him.

Roland Barthes speaks of the importance of the "already read," the *déjà lu*, in the ways we make sense of and respond to a new reading experience.[5] That "already read" informs our competence as readers, our capacity to understand and respond fully. In the case of *The Human Comedy*, the already read is built into the very structure of our reading. We open each new novel no longer innocent and naïve. We have a head start on these people—we know more about some of them than do the new characters called upon to interact with them. We are forewarned in a way those in the book cannot be. The more we read in *The Human Comedy*, the more masterful and sophisticated we feel. The fictive world fills in its outlines and reaches something like plenitude. Balzac in fact as he progressed and revised his earlier novels—and *The Human Comedy* is profoundly a product of revision, of after-writing to make the mosaic pieces fit, more or less, together—substitutes for real world figures his own invented ones. For instance, the real and famous poet Alphonse de Lamartine, mentioned frequently, fades away, erased by Melchior de Canalis, Balzac's invented poet who can represent the same kind of well-behaved Romantic poetry as Lamartine but also become a person in his own right, carrying out adventures that you couldn't very well attribute to such a well-known figure as Lamartine. By the time of *Modeste Mignon*, written in 1843, Canalis has become a famous poet with whom a young provincial girl can fall in love, and so narcissistic that he can tell his secretary to take care of the girl's love letters.

We may feel both comfortable and a bit crowded in Balzac's increasingly full world of fictive persons. They at times seem to take all the oxygen from the rooms in which they gather. In Chapter 3 I will talk about the novel Balzac started to write about an election in a provincial town, *The Member from Arcis* (*Le Député d'Arcis*), which he never finished, at least in part because the complicated interrelations of its characters had inspired him to go back to write their earlier history in *A Murky Business* (*Une ténébreuse affaire*). The weight of the past biographies and itineraries of his characters becomes as important as their present doings. We come to realize that power, in both a political sense and in the dynamic of personal relations, belongs to historical time. Power is like capital, an accumulation that you can spend sparingly or exorbitantly. And power is of course a key to how you get on in Balzac's world.

Power

Henry James, lover and fine expositor of Balzac, meditates in his later preface to his early novel *The American* on how he thought he was writing realism but in fact produced romance in that novel: "experience liberated, so to speak; experience disengaged, disembroiled, disencumbered, exempt from the conditions that we usually know to attach to it."[6] In reality, he now judges, his proud but impoverished French aristocrats, the Bellegardes, would have set aside their class prejudices to jump at Christopher Newman's millions. Then he reflects on his plot, which seems to put the Bellegardes eventually in Newman's power, and notes parenthetically:

> It is as difficult, I said above, to trace the dividing-line between the real and the romantic as to plant a milestone between north and south; but I am not sure an infallible sign of the latter is not this

rank vegetation of the "power" of bad people that good people
get into, or *vice versa*. It is so rarely, alas, into *our* power that
anyone gets!   (1067)

One could unpack James's sentence at almost infinite length,
especially because throughout his work, including the late and
most subtle of his novels, the manipulation of others, the illicit
exercise of power by one human being over another, is James's
profound subject. If he rejects his version of power in *The American*
as romantic rather than real, it is only because it is too overt and
stagey. It is what I think we could call melodramatic: precisely the
genre and the mode that wants the terms of power struggles, victimization, and the fight to recognize and reward persecuted
innocence, to be fully staged and articulated.

James's fiction owes much to Balzac (most clearly his early novels, but in more muted fashion his later ones too), and nowhere
more than in his understanding of power. For Balzac, power often
appears as the exercise of the will, conceived of as a kind of fluid
that can be concentrated and turned toward the dominance of
others. Two of his young protagonists, Raphaël de Valentin in *The
Fatal Skin* and the philosopher Louis Lambert, in *Louis Lambert*,
labor over treatises on the Will. Some of his visionaries seek a
kind of absolute knowledge that would allow them to accede to
domains of absolute power, most notably the chemist/alchemist
Balthasar Claës in *The Search for the Absolute (La recherche de l'Absolu)*.
Those who remain on the plane of more worldly exercises of
power may enhance their potency through secret societies, of
which there are several in *The Human Comedy*, notably The Thirteen,
les Treize, which groups a number of socially prominent men in
an all-for-each organization that multiplies their individual

17

forces. When General de Montriveau tells the recalcitrant Duchesse de Langeais, whom he is courting, that he can summon "a power more absolute than that of the czar of all the Russias," he doesn't exaggerate by much. His confederates of The Thirteen abduct Antoinette from a ball in the heart of Paris, and later penetrate into a convent to snatch her again—though at the last only as a dead body. There is also a secret society of beneficence in the Brothers of Consolation. And the underground convict organization known as *les Grands Fanandels*, the convict aristocracy, those who serve as the House of Lords for denizens of the underworld.

The master figure of power in *The Human Comedy* is Vautrin, alias Cheat-Death, alias Reverend Father Carlos Herrera, alias Jacques Collin—this last his "true" name that will emerge when he wishes it to, toward the end of his career when he decides he will no longer wage war against society but rather pass to the other side, to join the police and spend the rest of his career repressing what he earlier espoused. The very imagining of a superman such as Collin, who reappears again and again but always in disguise, his power always occult, poses most starkly questions about the nature of power to Balzac. Collin exercises his vast influence by mediation, through the beautiful young men he adopts: Colonel Franchessini, Rastignac, Lucien de Rubempré, Théodore Calvi. Power is most itself when you cannot see it, when it is hidden behind the arras of social form. Its exercise is felt rather than seen. It is wholly amoral. It is deeply erotic but it does not manifest itself as realized sexuality, which would lead to its depletion. Of all Collin's many extraordinary appearances through many novels, the one that maybe best sums up the nature of his power comes in the first part of *A Harlot High and Low* at the masked ball at the Opéra when Collin, masked, looking like a wild boar (which is what a *vautrin* is) speaks to Rastignac, telling him to see to it that Lucien, returned from his destitution and near suicide to Parisian life thanks to Collin become the Spanish priest Carlos Herrera, is accepted by Parisian social networks. When he hears the voice coming from behind the mask, Rastignac says: "It could only be *him*." To which Collin replies: "Act as if it were *him*." Obey, and don't ask questions.

Stories in *The Human Comedy* very often turn on the interaction of manipulators and manipulated. Someone is always getting into someone else's power. Love can easily be used to control another, as most strikingly in *The Marriage Contract (Le contrat de mariage)* and *The Black Sheep (La Rabouilleuse)* and *Cousin Bette (La cousine Bette)*, but really pervasively throughout Balzac's work. Money works too, of course, as Rastignac discovers when he enlists himself as Delphine de Nucingen's lover and becomes a useful player in her husband's financial legerdemain. James's "rank vegetation" of power relationships is everywhere in Balzac, and we will discover examples as we go along. The society that Balzac creates and reflects upon is undergoing major upheavals and profound transformations as it emerges from an old regime of assigned identities—identities you were born into—to a brave new world of achieved identities: identities that are up for grabs, that must be fought for and conquered, displayed and held on to against threats from others. The menace of exposure for assuming an identity that isn't one's own lurks everywhere. It wracks Lucien's life, first in his need to acquire legally the right to his mother's aristocratic name, de Rubempré, that he initially simply grabs without authorization, then later the need to gain a sound financial underpinning for the social status he simulates using funds that Collin apparently appropriated from a dying man he attended as supposed priest in Spain, maybe also money siphoned from the convicts' bank he is trustee for. Collin's convict identity is branded on his shoulder in the letters TF, for *Travaux Forcés*, forced labor, to which he was sentenced—yet which he has more or less succeeded in effacing through self-inflicted buckshot wounds. A less criminal but equally troubling case may be found in *Modeste Mignon,* where the secretary to the poet Canalis starts answering in the poet's name fan letters sent by Modeste Mignon, and the correspondence develops into an intense courtship underlain by a mistaken identity.

It's of course Collin who gives the theory of power exercised through others, in a version that sounds as if it might be benign:

> I wish to love my creature, mold him, shape him to my use, in order to love him as a father loves his child. I will ride in your tilbury, my boy. I will take pleasure in your successes with women, I will say: "This handsome young man, it's me! This Marquis de Rubempré, I created him and put him in aristocratic society; his greatness is my work, he speaks or falls silent with my voice, he consults me in everything!"[7]

This realizes common scenarios of Balzac's beloved *Arabian Nights*, where magical formulae allow someone to live within another. It resembles the power exercised by the aspiring young writer of *Facino Cane,* who tells us he has an ability to pass into the body and soul of other people, to espouse their very being. If Rastignac breaks away from the dependency entailed by Vautrin's plot for him, Lucien succumbs, and becomes a kind of hollowed-out person as he serves Collin's ambitions for him. Many of Henry James's plots seem designed precisely to work against such subservience.

Rastignac's Fortune

Let me close this chapter with a return to where I began, with Rastignac and *Père Goriot*. When that novel ends, we know that Rastignac's unsatisfied appetites will lead him to further adventures. We pick up from other novels allusions to his success, his access to both money and power. But we don't know the inner story of his acquisitiveness until we read *The House of Nucingen*, named for the bank of his lover's husband. Don't think this short novel will answer the question of how Rastignac made his fortune in any straightforward manner. It's one of Balzac's most inventive and audacious narratives, one that is reported by an unnamed narrator who has eavesdropped on it, overheard it through the partition between two private rooms in a famous Parisian restaurant, where he is dining with a woman he won't name out of discretion. Into the adjoining room come four men, *condottieri* of modern life: Andoche Finot and Emile Blondet, journalists we meet in *Lost Illusions*, the omnipresent caricaturist Jean-Jacques Bixiou, the disreputable *arriviste* Couture. It's this last who poses the question about Rastignac:

> "But how did he make his fortune," asked Couture. "In 1819, along with the illustrious Bianchon, he was in a miserable pension in the Latin Quarter; his family was eating roast grasshoppers and drinking homemade wine in order to be able to send him a hundred francs a month; his father's estate wasn't worth a thousand écus; he had two sisters and a brother on his shoulders, and now…"
>
> "Now he has forty thousand francs of dividends," Finot picked up; "each of his sisters has been richly dowered and nobly married, and he's left a life interest in the estate to his mother…"
>
> "In 1827," said Blondet, "I knew him still to be without a penny."

"Oh! in 1827," said Bixiou.

"And so," Finot continued, "today we see him on the way to becoming a member of the cabinet, peer of the realm, everything he could wish to be!"[8]

This kind of back-and-forth exchange continues, with enormous digressions and non-sequiturs that take us through many another story of notable young Parisian dandies, eventually to sketch how Rastignac unwittingly served as a front in a fraudulent bankruptcy staged by Nucingen that left several families destitute but brought the bank a whopping profit, some of it shared with Rastignac. I simplify a financial operation of enormous complication—it mirrors in the circulation of capital and stocks the indirection and baroque complication of the narration of The House of Nucingen itself. We discover the origins of Rastignac's fortune through a digressive conversation propelled by Couture's original question through several other personal dramas that all together tell us something about the new age of rapacious capitalist finance. The telling and the tale mirror one another, not in any obvious thematic way, more as an effect of our curiosity as readers. We are very much in the position of the original narrator who introduces the novel, eavesdropping through the partition between dining rooms. When at the end this first narrator and his partner leave their room, they are in their turn overheard.

"Hey, there were people in the next room," said Finot in hearing us go out.

"There are always people next door," replied Blondet, who must have been drunk.

The drunken wisdom of Blondet here bears thinking about. Are the best stories always not merely heard but overheard? Do we find out the secrets we want most to know, how the penniless law student of the Pension Vauquer became a millionaire on his way to the highest reaches of power, for instance, by listening to conversations of which we are not a part? Do we as readers enjoy eavesdropping, listening in to information not designed for our hearing? Balzac once again displays his masterful sense of what we as readers want from stories: access to a world we are normally cut off from. One of the great attractions of the novel over the ages has been its offer of information about people and institutions that we can't otherwise know. At its best, it allows us to be universal eavesdroppers, vouchsafed knowledge otherwise hidden, free from detection (until it's too late).

As for Rastignac, Bixiou sketches what he has become over time:

> he did not believe in any virtue, but rather in circumstances in which man is virtuous. This understanding was the matter of a moment: it was acquired at the height of Père-Lachaise cemetery, the day he buried a poor old honest man, the father of his Delphine, who died the dupe of society, of the truest emotions, abandoned by his daughters and his sons-in-law. He resolved to fool everybody in this society, and to present himself in the clothing of virtue, probity, and good manners. Egotism armed this young noble from head to foot.   (P 6:381/LB 15:491–2)

We are not of course required to accept Bixiou's estimate of Rastignac's character: it may be an extreme view, to be set next to less severe judgments. It sends the reader back to think about our first and abiding view of the young man at the outset of his career. When Vautrin tells him he has a way to get him the million he needs, and fast, Rastignac's first reaction is unnuanced: "'What do I have to do?' he said avidly, interrupting Vautrin." (P 3:142/S 114)

"Avidly"—it sounds a bit odd in English; *avidemment:* it's again that appetite, that need to devour the world orally, to ingest it. Rastignac will reject the form of satisfaction offered by Vautrin—the provision of Victorine Taillefer as bride after murdering her brother. That is too crude a solution to be digested at this point. But Vautrin tells him he'll do worse: he will find a way to use love to make himself money. And indeed that will be the story of his long liaison with Delphine de Nucingen, the perfect woman who allows him to say "love," not insincerely but meaning at the same time: money. *The House of Nucingen* allows us to see how the trick was turned.

But it's less Rastignac's later success that we remember him for than the youthful appetency. That's what drives our reading of *Père Goriot,* and something similar is at work throughout *The Human Comedy.* There is more on offer, more novels, more characters, more adventures—more reading. And once we've been hooked on the kind of nourishment he offers us, we can't very well stop. Our avidity keeps us going. Which is not to say that it's like eating junk food. If Balzac has moments where you think his power diminishes, where he seems to be cranking out pages to meet a publisher's demand, they are infrequent. Mostly our bingeing is satisfied with something of real substance, the creation of a fully peopled world that offers a true criticism of life: a superior understanding of the ways of the world and the dynamic forces driving modern society. That, as we will eventually explore, seems to me the principal glory of Balzac. The "more" he stimulates us to want and then supplies really tells us things we want to know. Our reading does not go unrewarded.

FANGS AND KISSES

Passion

Readers who don't ask for more, who stop devouring Balzac after two or three of the major novels, are likely to miss the shorter works, stories and novellas, where Balzac most seems to unleash his obsessions, and to explore intense states of being. This is especially true in the domain of love and sex. Tales such as *The Girl with the Golden Eyes (La Fille aux yeux d'or)*, *Sarrasine*, *The Duchesse de Langeais (La Duchesse de Langeais)*, *Massimila Doni*, *A Passion in the Desert (Une passion dans le désert)* stage situations obsessive, extreme, over-the-top that in turn illuminate some more reticent or implied moments of the full-length novels. As Marcel Proust recognized, Balzac dares open to thought realms of sexuality normally repressed in the novel.[1] In doing so, he creates some remarkable women.

Take *A Passion in the Desert* as first example. The title presents a puzzling oxymoron: how do you find passion in the desert, by definition devoid of life? The story will tell of a French soldier captured by Maghrebis during Napoleon's Egyptian campaign, then escaping to wander lost in the desert. But it begins with a framing incident set in Paris, with a man and a woman at Monsieur Martin's menagerie (a really existing Paris attraction), observing Martin working his wild beasts. The woman exclaims on how Martin has won his animals' affection so he is able to go among them unharmed. The man replies that it's natural, and goes on to tell of how at his first visit to Martin's he was sitting next to an old army veteran with an amputated leg who responded to the wild animal act with a world-weary "Same old story."[2] Curious, the man invites the old soldier to lunch, where he tells his story—which the man then writes out for his woman friend. And that's the story that is transmitted to us.

Lost in the desert, the soldier eventually came upon an oasis, complete with a water hole, palm trees laden with dates, and a grotto in which he decided to spend the night. Awoken in the night by the rasping sound of breathing, he discovers he shares the grotto with a panther. It's too close for him to position his rifle to shoot it. As he waits for the panther to awake—and a possible mortal combat—he indulges in what may at first seem a pointless description:

> It was a female. The fur of the white belly and thighs glimmered. Several little velvety spots formed pretty bracelets around the paws. The muscular tail was also white but tipped with back rings. The upper part of the coat, yellow as matte gold but very smooth and soft, bore those characteristic spots shaped like roses that distinguish panthers from other kinds of *felis*. (P 8:1224/ NY 147)

Then the panther awakes:

> At last she yawned, displaying the fearsome array of her teeth and her grooved tongue, as hard as a grater. "She's like a little mistress!" thought the Frenchman, seeing her rolling around and making the gentlest, most flirtatious movements. (P 8:1225/NY 148)

We must make the connection that the text leaves tacit: the manner in which the fearsome mouth provokes the soldier's identification of her as a little mistress.

When the panther approaches, he caresses her and scratches her back. "The beast voluptuously raised her tail, her eyes softened…" And here begins a love story, motivated at first by the soldier's fear, his need to keep the panther always purring from pleasure. "'How demanding she is!' cried the Frenchman, smiling. He tried playing with her ears, caressing her belly, and scratching her head hard with his nails. And seeing his success, he tickled her skull with the point of his dagger, on the lookout for the moment to kill her; but the hardness of her bones made him tremble at the thought of failure." (P 8:1226/NY149) The temptation to strike the panther continues, but it is more and more subsumed into love games all the more arousing from the constant threat of danger. "He took her paws, her muzzle, he twisted her ears, rolled her onto her back, and scratched her warm, silky flanks hard. She participated willingly…" (P 8:1227–8/NY 150). He recalls his first mistress, whom he ironically nicknamed "Mignonne" because she was so much the opposite of that, so violently jealous that he feared she would knife him. So he names the panther Mignonne, and she comes to respond to his calls. When one night he attempts to flee her and the oasis, she chases him—and rescues him from a quicksand bog. From now on they belong to one another. Their days pass in caresses, they sleep side by side at night. He discovers she is jealous when his attention is distracted by a soaring eagle: his former mistress's soul must have passed into her body. "There was such youth and grace in her shape! She was as pretty as a woman. The blond fur of her coat was matched by the delicate tint of matte white tones that colored her thighs. The profuse light from the sun made that vivid gold and those brown spots shine with ineffable allure…. 'She has a soul,' he said…"

What we have, then, is a kind of criss-crossing discourse that describes the panther as if she were a woman, and at the same time suggests the description of woman as panther. Naming the panther "Mignonne" ironically, or as the French says *"par antiphrase,"* opposite its accepted meaning, suggests the rhetorical strategy at work here. He can play sexually with the panther, caressing her thighs and scratching her belly, in ways that could not be represented in mainstream (non-pornographic) literature were she a woman. The antiphrastic discourse permits of a running commentary not only on the feline as womanly but also on woman as feline. Mignonne is at once desirable and fearsome, and the two qualities are inseparable. Her devouring mouth with its array of teeth (which appear often stained with blood from a recent kill) can't but recall the legendary *vagina dentata* of myth and folklore, alluring and castrating. The excessive jealousy of the soldier's human mistress transposed into the panther becomes something well beyond petty annoyance, a kind of total fidelity by which soldier and panther must live locked together in a relation of passion (as the title of the story puts it) that is at once full of arousal and fear.

The climax of the story fully realizes the antiphrastic discourse. The soldier's telling of his tale breaks off just after his statement that Mignonne has a soul: "'She has a soul…,' he said, studying the perfect calm of this queen of the sands, gilded like them, white like them, solitary and burning like them…" Then we have the reaction of the first narrator's woman friend to her reading of the story he has written out from the soldier's oral tale: "'So then,' she said to me, 'I've read your pleading in favor of animals, but how did it end between two persons so well suited to understand each other?'" And here the first narrator is obliged to deliver the ending which he appears to have censored from his written version: "They ended the way all grand passions do, by a misunderstanding." Giving his companion the end of the tale, he says, is "horribly difficult." It seems that the soldier does something that hurts her—he didn't mean to—and the panther turns on him and "with her sharp teeth she bit my leg, weakly no doubt." Is this an attack on the part of the panther, or a caress? The soldier, "believing that she wanted to devour me," plunges his dagger into her throat. "She rolled over letting out a cry that froze my heart. I saw her struggling while looking at me without anger. I would have given anything in the world, even the Legion of Honor that I didn't yet have, to bring her back to life. It was as if I had murdered a real person." (P 8:1232/NY 154–5)

The danger of sex with the panther in the end takes an S/M relation over the brink, to murder—though with the instantaneous recognition that this wasn't what he meant, and seemingly not what she meant either. It's simply passion run away with itself. At Mignonne's death, he is ready to call her "a real person," to allow her to enter the discourse of real woman, no longer only an antiphrasis. But the tale is not quite done. We learn that just after the killing of Mignonne, the soldier is rescued by soldiers who've seen the flag he flies from a palm tree. They find him in tears. He concludes with an evocation of the desert, "where there is everything and there is nothing." Asked to explain, he says: "it is God without men."

This desert sublimity, we may surmise, has something to with the irreproducible passion he encountered there. Recall that when the narrator first meets him, the soldier is described as having lost his right leg to amputation. Did this have anything to do with the panther's bite? Perhaps not, since he tells us that after Egypt he fought in Germany and Spain and Russia. But its unexplained origin does suggest symbolically the price of love with the panther, the results of sex with a woman so fiercely armed with teeth, and with her phallic tail, as well as her silky thighs and tender belly. It's not made explicit, as indeed it can't be since the soldier's desert passion, though told in the straightforward prose of realism, is nearly an allegory of a certain fantasy of male–female relations. Love for a woman, claims the allegory, is at once alluring and dangerous. Its climax is all-destroying. You live on to regret it forever, but your very body is marked by it.

It's an astonishing tale, one of those extended moments where you think Balzac must be writing from his preconscious, in the nighttime silence when he did most of his writing, relaxing the work of the censor and spinning out a tale that is perfectly convincing while it is perfectly hallucinatory. Balzac explores extreme borders of passion in other tales; the best known is probably *The Girl with the Golden Eyes,* where the dandy Henri de Marsay is invited by a pair of grotesque servants to an adventure with a woman who lives sequestered within a Paris townhouse (to which he is led blindfolded), in a seashell-shaped room decorated in red, white, and gold with a fifty-foot divan in the middle. His lovemaking with Paquita is sublimely ecstatic: curiously, he finds she is at once virgin and expert in sex. Yet there comes a moment when the "error" in which "an iron hand" holds her ends: " 'Dead!' she said! 'I am dead!'…take me away to the ends of the earth, to an island where no one knows us.' "[3] This appears to be her reaction to discovery of the phallic love of which she has been kept in ignorance. Her sessions with Henri are passionate, but then at a moment of orgasm she calls out: "Oh! Mariquita!" A moment of painful illumination for de Marsay: he realizes that she has had a woman lover, and he is wounded in his phallic pride. Paquita doesn't understand why; Henri nonetheless vows vengeance. But when he returns with henchmen for this purpose, he finds he has been anticipated by Paquita's lover and keeper, the Marquise de San-Réal.

Paquita is expiring in a pool of blood, her body marked by stab wounds, while the Marquise, half naked, her breasts scratched, her hair loose, bleeding from bite wounds, stands over her with a dagger. "She was sublime thus." (P 5:1107/O 136). When she becomes aware of Henri's entrance, she runs at him with the dagger. He arrests her hand. Then they look closely at one another, horror turning the blood in their veins to ice. They look like twins. They speak at the same moment, the same words: "Lord Dudley must be your father?" (P 5:1108/O 136). (This English lord, a minor figure in *The Human Comedy,* has spawned children more or less everywhere.) They are half siblings. This prompts Henri to remark, pointing to the blood-stained corpse of Paquita: "She was faithful to the blood." A kind of macabre joke, which tells us that Paquita's lovers were essentially the same person in a different gender. And now Henri suggests that they must see each other again. To which the Marquise, Margarita, replies: "No, brother…we will never see each other again. I am returning to Spain, to enter the convent of Los Dolores." And Henri, addressing her in the intimate *tu:* "'You are still too young, too beautiful,' said Henri, taking her in his arms and kissing her." But she has the last word: "'Farewell,' she said, 'there is no consolation for having lost what seemed like the infinite.'" So that at the end there is a whiff of possible incest, at least half-incest, refused because the Marquise's same-sex love had produced an infinite that de Marsay can't match. There is something beyond male-female coupling that de Marsay, the beautiful man, can never understand or attain to.

The Girl with the Golden Eyes is a truly audacious story, as Proust claimed: like Vautrin's relations with his young male protégés, it opens to literary representation same-sex love generally kept in the literary closet or underworld. It also literalizes a Romantic trope of fraternal-sororal incest as the perfect coupling—almost like coupling with one self, though with sexual difference—making good on François-René de Chateaubriand's scenario in his tale *René*, and on other instances where the perfect mating is incestuous, a tradition extended by Wagner with Siegmund and Sieglinde in *Die Walküre*, brother and sister who engender the hero Siegfried. Wagner may help to make the point that most Romantic longing for incest plays out in fantasy or in the realm of legendary beings. Balzac makes it happen, almost, in present-day Paris. His story also casts doubt on the claims for the primacy of the phallus urged not only by de Marsay but by the entire male cast in his novels, as in the world outside them. The Marquise de San-Réal, sexy as can be in her brief blood-stained appearance, will have none of that prejudice.

You might move from this story of passion to the simulation of passion that really covers over vengeance and venality with the team of Valérie Marneff and Lisbeth Fischer in *Cousin Bette (La cousine Bette)*. Here sex is weaponized. Valérie, backed and urged on by Bette, creates ravages throughout society. They are made possible by the incurable lechery of men, notably Baron Hulot, who destroys his family, steals money from the State, causes the suicide of an honorable uncle, causes his wife's death, and eventually, in his seventies, marries a plump Norman servant.

Sex in Balzac is a powerful force. When it comes to the young, as to Lucien de Rubempré when he goes to bed with the "delicious" actress Coralie, to begin a relationship that will destroy them both, or to the lonely Félix de Vandenesse when he discovers the bare shoulders of Henriette de Mortsauf at a ball and can't help kissing them, igniting a painful relation of desire aroused and repressed, sex is life-altering. In a satiric vein, the soul sold to the devil in *Melmoth Reconciled (Melmoth réconcilié)* exercises fiendish power over whoever possesses it until a young clerk uses it to gain access to the courtisane Euphrasie and in a twelve-day sexual orgy exhausts its power. But it is not only about men. *The Woman of Thirty (La femme de trente ans)* explores the disappointments and woundings of marital sex from a woman's point of view: the ineptitude and lack of interest in a woman's sexual needs and desires on the part of an obtuse and somewhat brutal husband. And in contrast to the sad marriage of Julie d'Aiglemont stands the story of her daughter Hélène, who runs off with a pirate and experiences the joys of sexual satisfaction, though she will come to a sad end. Other examples come in *The Memoirs of Two Young Wives (Mémoires de deux jeunes mariées)*, an epistolary novel where two young women emerging from the same convent school correspond with one another about their experiences of love, marriage, childbirth (and birth control), family, and the possibilities of passion, which one of them renounces for bourgeois comfort, and the other pursues. In *Béatrix*, Balzac creates a tortured set of love relationships that make his principal actors "galley slaves of love," unable to escape from its alluring and painful bonds. Balzac won his woman readership through such explorations of what it might be like to be a woman, subject to the limits set on a woman's freedom of action in society, and the costs of attempts to break with convention. Many women readers wrote to him, expressing their need to disburden themselves of their marital sufferings and the silence imposed upon them.[4] The most famous critic of the time,

Charles Augustin Sainte-Beuve, accused Balzac of a kind of unhealthy interest in women's private lives: he conquered his feminine public, says Sainte-Beuve, though its infirmities, like a plague.[5]

The Swan

Balzac's most heroic woman—and I think the one he loves most—stands out for her exceptionalism, her refusal of modernity and its limitations. She eventually dominates the novel in which she figures, though this takes a while. The novel is *A Murky Business (Une ténébreuse affaire)*. I first read it many years ago more out of a sense of duty than anything else—I wanted to know the earlier machinations of the police spies Corentin and Peyrade, who play a large role in *A Harlot High and Low*. One more instance of how reading a single Balzac novel creates the wish and the need for more, to fill up gaps in the lives of characters, to satisfy the desire to know them more fully. But I think I was too confused by the tortuous plot to appreciate it fully. Now I am ready to agree with the poet Paul Valéry (who basically disliked novels) that it is one of Balzac's masterpieces. Let's see: you need to know that the plot turns on Michu, a kind of human bulldog whose father was public executioner in the town of Troyes, in the Champagne region, during the Reign of Terror: Michu is considered to be a Jacobin whereas at heart he is loyal to the monarchy and the local aristocracy, and secretly hopes to restore lands confiscated from the Hauteserre and Simeuse families during the Revolution. These lands now belong to Malin de Gondreville, a slippery and successful political figure who becomes a senator in the Napoleonic regime. Michu will eventually pay with his life for his devotion to the nobles, who are equally loyal to him. Monsieur and Madame d'Hauteserre are moderates who have accepted the Napoleonic regime and wish to live peacefully in their country chateau—their townhouse in Troyes was attacked during the Revolution—while their sons Robert and Adrien serve in the Army of the Princes, émigré aristocrats who have refused loyalty to Napoleon's rule, along with their Simeuse cousins, the identical twins Marie-Paul and Paul-Marie.

Laurence de Cinq-Cygne, orphaned when her parents died on the guillotine following the attack on the family mansion in Troyes, raised by her uncle M. d'Hauteserre, bears a name so honored that it can be transmitted through women: the man who marries Laurence will become Comte de Cinq-Cygne. The name derives from five young blonde women who long ago defended the family seat from an attack, and became known as the Five Swans. Their motto has been passed on with the name: "To Sing While Dying." At age twenty-three, Laurence has the delicate and virginal appearance of a swan whereas she holds within her an iron will and has learned to ride and to handle guns with all the force and ability of a man.

> The warrior was hidden under the most feminine and fragile appearance. Her heart was excessively tender, but she carried in her head a virile determination and a stoic resistance. Her farseeing eyes did not hold tears. To look at her delicate wrist shaded by blue veins, no one would have guessed that it could challenge that of the most hardened horseman. Her hand, so soft and fluid, handled a pistol and a rifle with the vigor of an experienced hunter. On the outside, she was always in the fashion of a lady dressed to ride, with a cute little beaver hat with a veil over her face.[6]

Balzac creates in Laurence something of an Amazon, but one whose appearance on the contrary is all femininity: she is, like so many of the women he appreciates, a bit of an androgyne. She is in love but with the restraint of the proper young virgin, and in a manner that well corresponds to her androgyny: in love with both of the Simeuse twins, without finding any way to choose between them. It's in fact as if she needed them both to satisfy what we divine will be her fierce sexual appetite once it is allowed expression.

Laurence is always on horseback, sometimes covering fifteen leagues (about sixty kilometers) in a day, accompanied by a young peasant, Gothard, whom she has trained to be her groom, messenger, and spy. In fact, the Hauteserre brothers and the Simeuse twins are not off in Germany with the royalist armies. They have returned to France to take part in a plot to overthrow Napoleon and restore the Bourbon monarchy. We are in 1803, when Napoleon has consolidated power as First Consul but hasn't yet been crowned Emperor. It's Joseph Fouché, Napoleon's chief of police (not a figure imagined by Balzac but a real and powerful historical actor) who has sent Corentin and Peyrade into the region precisely because he fears such a plot. Laurence has held meetings with the four gentlemen, as they are most often called; now they are on the way to Paris, on this dangerous mission. If caught, they will be executed.

Corentin and Peyrade enlist the local gendarmerie to surround the Château de Cinq-Cygne, and the two detectives enter to search for any illicit persons. M. et Mme d'Hauteserre and their friend the abbé Gouget, once tutor to the Simeuse brothers, and his sister Mlle Gouget, are engaged in their nightly card game when the detectives arrive. Laurence escapes at the last minute, warned by

Michu's wife Marthe, and joins Michu in the forest. He then leads her to the hideaway that will play a central role in the story: in forest of Nodesme lie the ruins of an old monastery, overgrown with brush but with an underground grotto that is inhabitable, next to a spring-fed pond for water supply. Michu gallops off to warn the four gentlemen that their part in the plot is known, and that they must not enter Paris; they will in fact come back to the forest of Nodesme, to be hidden in Michu's grotto. Then Laurence returns to the château and confronts Corentin: "the two true adversaries" now face one another (P 8:580/P 104). Corentin is holding a small casket he has taken from her bedroom. Laurence attacks him with her riding crop, he drops the casket, which she then throws in the fire. Corentin manages to retrieve the burning box, and in it finds a letter from the Simeuse parents to Laurence written on the eve of their execution on the guillotine, locks of their white hair, letters of eternal love from Marie-Paul and Paul-Marie, and, in the hidden compartment of the casket, their miniature portraits. Abbé Goujet is astonished that Laurence has been willing to sacrifice these precious relics. Laurence shrugs her shoulders in response, and Goujet suddenly realizes that she is ready to sacrifice anything and everything to gain time for the four noblemen to reach safety. He lifts his eyes admiringly to heaven.

Laurence wins this round of the battle against Corentin. The young conspirators, spend seven months sequestered in the grotto, and then apparently are pardoned by Napoleon and removed from the list of the proscribed. They emerge to live at the Château de Cinq-Cygne, despite the warnings of their old uncle, the Marquis de Chargeboeuf, that they still have powerful enemies. Comes a feast day, when they decide to send all the servants off to the fête in Troyes, while the four young men, along with Michu and Laurence, at last dig up the hidden Simeuse treasure, buried in the forest, and bring it back to the château. This turns out to be the same day that Corentin and Peyrade capture Malin de Gondreville, and as part of their plot against the Cinq-Cygne and Simeuse clan, hide him in the same grotto used by the four gentlemen, which the detectives have finally discovered. Meanwhile, Laurence and Marie-Paul and Paul-Marie during their day at work unburying the treasure have decided that the time has come to resolve who will become Laurence's husband. They decide to let this undecidable question be resolved by chance: the first one of the twins to whom Madame d'Hauteserre addresses a word at dinner that night will become her husband. That momentous choice is just about to take place when the police arrive to arrest the Simeuse twins, the Hauteserre brothers, and Michu: they are now accused of having kidnapped Malin de Gondreville. Corentin has now won round two.

The scene now shifts to the courtroom, and various machinations to prove that the accused are innocent, as in fact this time they are. But circumstantial evidence is all against them—their trip into the forest to retrieve their hidden gold can be interpreted as an expedition to kidnap Malin. There is apparent motive for this since after the Revolution he seized the property of Gondreville that had been in the Cinq-Cygne family. Michu is framed by an additional trick of Corentin's, a forged note apparently in his hand instructing his wife Marthe to bring supplies to the secret grotto, falsely proving that Michu masterminded the kidnapping. When the jury returns, all are found guilty, the Simeuse twins sentenced to twenty-four years of hard labor, the Hauteserre brothers to ten years, and Michu to death.

Swan and Imperial Eagle

All this prepares Laurence's sublime moment. The only recourse left her is to plead for clemency from that Napoleon she has spurned as a usurper, never to be accepted as legitimate ruler of France. He now is Emperor, having crowned himself at the Cathedral of Notre-Dame in the presence of Pope Pius VII in 1804. As a noblewoman who always believed Napoleon a wrongful occupier of the throne that rightfully belongs to the Bourbons, Laurence finds the idea of bending her knee to Napoleon humiliating beyond belief. But she is ready to do anything to save her cousins. So armed with a letter from the Minister of Foreign Affairs, the famous Talleyrand, in the company of her old uncle Chargeboeuf, she sets out for Prussia. We are on the eve of the battle of Jena, which will prove to be a decisive French victory. As they approach the scene of operations, Laurence finds herself thrilled by the troop movements to which she is witness, the splendor of the uniforms, the sense of historic forces in play, and she conceives an admiration for the mind animating these masses of men. Then she perceives the man of destiny himself, on horseback, giving orders to his generals. She is astonished at his simplicity.

Napoleon has established his bivouac on a plateau overlooking what will on the morrow be the battlefield of Jena. From these heights, to the onlookers Laurence and Chargeboeuf, "the majesty of war stood out in all its splendor" (P 8:680/P 207). They see the battle lines of the two armies lit by the moon. Aides come and go around them incessantly. Finally they are admitted to the Emperor's presence in the rude thatch-roofed cabin that is his headquarters. He has just finished dining, and sits at a table with a map open before him, as in a painting that might be titled: the general on the eve of battle. It's in fact a kind of ekphrastic moment, as if describing a painted portrait of the man of destiny:

> Napoleon was seated in a rustic chair. His boots, covered with mud, bore witness to his goings and comings across the fields. He had taken off his well-known overcoat, and his famous green uniform, slashed by the red silk of his decoration, put in relief below by the white of his cashmere trousers and his vest, showed to admirable advantage his pale and terrible Caesar's face. (P 8:680/P 207–8)

He asks Laurence if she doesn't fear to speak to him on the eve of battle. She states who she is, and falls to her knees, offering him the petition written by Talleyrand. Now the Emperor lifts her "gracefully" to her feet, "with a knowing glance" and asks: "Will you finally be good? Do you understand the meaning of the French Empire?" And at this point comes Laurence's conversion, in a moment that mimics the heroism of Pierre Corneille's *Cinna*, where the Emperor Caesar Augustus pardons those who conspired against him. "Ah, at this moment I understand only the Emperor," Laurence replies, overcome by the great good humor with which Napoleon has spoken to her, and foreseeing his grant of pardon.

"Are they innocent?" the Emperor asks her. "All," she replies. Napoleon demurs: Michu is a dangerous man. If you had such a faithful friend devoted to you, would you abandon him? she asks in return. "You're a woman," Napoleon replies, with a touch of mockery. "'And you a man of iron!' she answered him, with an impassioned hardness that pleased him." They continue to disagree about Michu's guilt or innocence.

And now the Emperor takes Laurence by the hand and leads her outside on the plateau overlooking the battlefield.

"Look," he said to her in the voice that could transform the cowardly into the brave, "there are three hundred thousand men, they too are innocent! Well then, tomorrow thirty thousand of them will be dead, dying for their countries! Perhaps there is among the Prussians a great engineer, a great philosopher, a genius who will be cut down. On our side, we will certainly lose great men unknown. And maybe I will see my best friend killed. Will I cry out against God? No. I will be silent. Know then, Mademoiselle, that one must die for the laws of one's country just as one dies here for her glory," he added, leading her back into the hut. "Be off, go back to France," he said, looking toward Chargeboeuf. "My orders will follow."

Laurence thought he had granted a commutation of Michu's sentence, and in the emotion of her gratitude she bent her knee and kissed the Emperor's hand.   (P 8:681–2/P 209)

The next day Laurence and Chargeboeuf take the road back to France as one hundred cannon growl, opening the battle that will end with Napoleon's complete and astonishing victory.

The scene between Laurence and Napoleon, charged with a suppressed eros, marks a highpoint in her career, a kind of *image d'Epinal* moment, a scene to be preserved in an etching, under glass. Story and History converge. It is hagiographic in its presentation of Napoleon as "man of iron": Laurence, though his caste enemy, from a family that rejects all that has happened since the first moment of the French Revolution, responds to his visible, palpable greatness, falling on her knees, kissing his hand. His lesson to her as they look down on the morrow's battlefield on which so many young men of future potential will perish is something for a child's illustrated history book. It's like those defining historical moments chosen for illustration by Delacroix in his history paintings, or those that Sartre's characters Roquentin and Annie, in *La Nausée,* identify as "perfect moments."[7] It is a moment that exemplifies and illustrates.

And like the fictional and historical protagonists who meet here, it is sublime.

And yet it is deceptive as well. When a week later Laurence and her uncle reach Troyes, an order has been issued to free the four gentlemen, the Simeuse twins and the Hauteserre brothers, on parole, along with the order to proceed immediately with Michu's execution. Laurence has been fooled: the Emperor's magnificence has deceived her into believing in a munificence that has turned out to be only partial. Laurence at once goes to see Michu in his cell. He understands that it is fated that the guard dog must die at the place his original masters, the Simeuse parents, were put to death. She remains with him as the guards prepare him for the guillotine. He asks if he might have permission to kiss her hand; she instead holds out her face, to allow herself to be kissed "in saintly manner" by this noble victim.

No sooner has Michu been guillotined than an orderly arrives with commissions as second lieutenant in the same regiment for the four gentlemen. They are to leave at once to join their troops. Their parting from Laurence is devastating; it's as if they have a foreboding of the future. Laurence returns alone to the empty château. Now the narrative reaches its outcomes swiftly. Marie-Paul and Paul-Marie die together at the battle of Sommo-Sierra, in 1808, the one defending the other, crying out: "Laurence, here I die!" Robert, the elder d'Hauteserre brother, dies at the battle of Moskova; his younger brother Adrien is gravely wounded at the battle of Dresden, and manages to return to Cinq-Cygne to recover. Laurence, now thirty-two, marries him in order to salvage the family line: she offers him a "withered heart, which he accepted." (P 8:684/P 211)

Comes the Restoration of the Bourbons that Laurence so ardently and heroically worked for, but she reacts without enthusiasm: it has come too late for her. Adrien accumulates all the honors that can be bestowed on a faithful royalist, and dies in 1829 in the arms of Laurence, his father, and his adoring children. Laurence raises Michu's son as if he were her own. He is admitted to the bar in 1817, then becomes judge, and finally royal prosecutor in nearby Arcis in 1827. Laurence has carefully invested the funds left by Michu, and is able to give the son an income of twelve thousand pounds when he turns twenty-one, and later arranges his marriage to the rich Mademoiselle Girel of Troyes. One has the sense of her posthumous loyalty to the family "guard dog" as the most important emotional strand in her life following the debacle.

The novel appears to be over. But we are offered a brief conclusion that does two things: it elucidates (to a degree: this is a murky business) the kidnapping of Malin de Gondreville, who had at that point returned to his château (once the possession of the Cinq-Cygne family) to burn highly incriminating papers dating from the moment in 1800 when he was part of an earlier plot to overthrow Bonaparte, then a young general fighting in Italy—a plot abandoned when Bonaparte gained a notable victory at the battle of Marengo, and then returned swiftly to France to reclaim his authority as First Consul. That plot was initiated and directed by Fouché, the powerful, long-serving, and sinister chief of police. But the later plot to frame and destroy the Cinq-Cygne family, serving a long-standing resentment against the irreconcilable partisans of the Bourbons, its animus against the Cinq-Cygne family, seems to have been brought to white heat by a single gesture: Laurence's striking the agent Corentin with her riding crop. Thus do major historical events turn on private personal insults.

We learn also of Laurence's later existence in the magnificent Paris hôtel her husband purchased. We're now under the bourgeois monarchy of Louis-Philippe, following the Revolution of 1830, whom she, like a true Faubourg Saint-German aristocrat, does not recognize as a legitimate ruler. She had learned to love the faithful Adrien in later life. Now, alone with her children, she lives a serene existence, though over her fireplace hangs a portrait painted by Robert Lefebvre—of Michu in prison. Her daughter Berthe is the living portrait of her mother, but without her warlike audacity—"more womanly," as Laurence describes her. We discover that the Princesse de Cadignan, another proud aristocrat whose somewhat notorious past—many love affairs—has been superseded by a pious old age, hopes to marry her son Georges de Maufrigneuse to Berthe. She makes the error of including in her evening reception Henri de Marsay, now prime minister under Louis-Philippe—Laurence finds his presence shocking to her Legitimist principles, but accepts him as a man of good society nevertheless. But then the entry of the Comte Malin de Gondreville is announced: her old antagonist whose kidnapping and sequestration caused the trial of the four gentlemen and Michu, and in the long run the death of four of those five. He is now an indispensable part of the twelfth different regime he has served since 1789: one of those political veterans with developed survival skills, and zero moral scruples. Laurence promptly leaves the salon with Berthe, calculating her path to avoid meeting Gondreville. Has his unexpected arrival caused the marriage plans to collapse? Everyone understands the meaning of her departure, and they treat Gondreville with such disdain that he gets the message and leaves himself. It's at this point that de Marsay fills in the past story of Fouché, Gondreville, and Corentin.

Laurence will live on, a political force still in her château de Cinq-Cygne when it comes to the election, in 1839, recounted in *The Member from Arcis (Le député d'Arcis)*, the sequel novel Balzac actually began before writing *A Murky Business* but never completed. He in fact broke off writing it to go back to fill in the past that hangs over all the political maneuvering in Arcis. And then the background novel, *A Murky Business*, took on its own substance, and in the development of Laurence de Cinq-Cygne clearly captured the novelist's creative imagination far beyond the novel to which it was supposed to be a prequel.

The whole of *A Murky Business* is a breathless and intriguing story, something verging on a thriller but with an important historical and social import. It is the figure of Laurence as a kind of living swan who is also an Amazon that raises its plot above the ordinary and gives it a special aura. The scene in which she confronts Napoleon remains indelible in my reading of the novel. Only a fictional character of such grandeur could confront the historic man of destiny. Balzac clearly takes a risk here: putting Napoleon on stage as a principal character, someone who moves and speaks and interacts with fictional characters, takes audacity, and might easily fail. But Balzac beings it off, as a nearly Shakespearean moment, I think because Laurence as a character achieves the elevation needed to play opposite the Emperor. Her audacity matches Balzac's. I mentioned in passing that the scene evokes for me the climax of Corneille's *Cinna*, familiar to any French reader, where the Emperor Augustus pardons the man who plotted against him. Augustus calls upon Cinna to become his friend. And then he celebrates his own victory over the temptation to retaliation and punishment as an exemplary act, one that will live on in future history:

> *O siècles, ô mémoire!*
> *Conservez à jamais ma dernière victoire!*
>
> (O centuries, o memory!
> Preserve forever my final victory!)[8]

Laurence and Napoleon together achieve something of the sublimity of Cornelian drama, which most often turns on a protagonist's search to define and illustrate his or her *gloire,* a glory that comes from overcoming the limitations of flesh and social role to declare one's self-mastery and, by that fact, one's mastery of the world. As Augustus says when he arrives at his decision to pardon rather than punish:

> *Je suis maître de moi comme de l'univers;*
> *Je le suis, je veux l'être.*
>
> (I am master of myself as I am of the universe;
> I am master, I want to be master.)[9]

The being and the willing that stand in a reversed order here should I think be conceived as simultaneous: you become master of yourself by willing to be master. And by that act you are also master of the universe. That is of course Napoleon's wish and his achievement. But it characterizes Laurence as well. She is supremely master of herself, a being characterized by her voluntarism. Even the diminished eros of her marriage to Adrien d'Hauteserre represents an act of will, a determination that the Cinq-Cygne line will continue—its name passed on through women, its title conferred on husbands by their wives.

Laurence, you could say, is as much a fantasy as the panther of *A Passion in the Desert* or the sequestered and sexy Paquita of *The Girl with the Golden Eyes*. She is the phallic woman and the virgin, destined to fulfill fantasies of a male warrior companion who is in fact female, with whom you could have sex if you were chosen to do so. The fact that neither Marie-Paul nor Paul-Marie gets to have sex with Laurence perhaps signals her ultimate inaccessibility. When she finally marries Adrien she has lost her eros: it's a marriage of reason. But in that marriage she is kind, gentle, an attentive wife and loving mother. She has none of the predatory traits of the panther or such pantherish women as Lisbeth Fischer and Valérie Marneffe, or others such as Flore Brazier in *The Black Sheep* (*La Rabouilleuse*) who use their sexuality to entrap and destroy men and gain fortunes. Laurence is alone of all her sex among Balzac's women, though her virtues and her misfortunes evoke such as Henriette de Mortsauf in *The Lily of the Valley* or Claire de Beauséant in *Père Goriot* and *The Abandoned Woman* or Louise de Chaulieu in *Memoirs of Two Young Wives*. There are not many happy women in *The Human Comedy*, and Balzac is a keen analyst of the problem: in essence, patriarchy and its institutionalization in marriage.

Julie d'Aiglemont in *The Woman of Thirty* gives a lucid account of the state of woman in society as it has been constituted—by men—in her conversation with a priest, who tells her she needs to obey the laws of society:

> "Obey society?…" replied the Marquise, with a gesture of horror. "But Monsieur, all our ills come from that. God has not decreed a law of unhappiness, but in coming together men have falsified his work. We are, as women, more mistreated by civilization than we would be by nature.…Marriage, the institution on which society rests, today, makes us alone feel all its weight: for men there is

freedom, for women duties. We owe you our entire life, you owe us of yours only rare moments. Men make a choice where we submit blindly. Oh, Monsieur, to you I can say everything. Well then, marriage as it is practiced today seems to me legal prostitution. That's where my suffering comes from…"[10]

The indictment is on target, and it is displayed in the situation of many a woman in Balzac's world who doesn't have Julie's analytic understanding of her position. It is one of Laurence's virtues that she escapes the passive obedience of marriage, never submits to its prostitution. To be sure she has to settle in the end for the diminished eros of marriage to Adrien, but at least her submission is a conscious choice, and what she chooses becomes an arena in which she can work out a new definition of her identity.

There would be so much more to say, for instance about a woman such as Esther van Gobseck, the most beautiful of them all, a prostitute redeemed by her love for Lucien de Rubempré who is obliged to sacrifice herself for his future happiness and gains her own form of sublimity in the "irony" with which she watches with lucid mind the forced sex her body must perform. And also about Antoinette de Langeais, waked from her numbed erotic life too late to find happiness. Or Henriette de Mortsauf, who maintains her virtue despite her husband's viciousness and the temptation offered by her would-be lover, only to discover at the end of her life that she may have made the wrong choice. As she writes to her young admirer, Félix de Vandenesse, in the letter he reads only after her death: "Do you still today remember your kisses? They have dominated my life. They cut a furrow through my soul. The ardor of your blood awakened the ardor of mine; your youth penetrated mine, your desires entered into my heart."[11] The memory trace set up by those kisses has dictated her life unto death. "Virtue" is not easy for any of these women. It is part of the rules dictated by men, to which women have been obliged to submit, and which their bodies and souls cry out against.

I have spoken at length of these fictional women because they make up such a large and vital part of my experience in reading Balzac. They have a kind of independent and vibrant existence despite their often limited freedom for action. When in his *General Introduction (Avant-Propos)* of *The Human Comedy* Balzac takes on the mantle of zoologist and compares the human species to the animal kingdom, he notes that with most animals once you have described the male of the species you need only say a few additional words about the female. But the situation with humans is totally different. The woman and the man may be completely mismatched: someone who should be a princess may be married to a butcher, and so on. So the feminine demands a separate description and analysis from the masculine. The problem with the model novelist he otherwise adores, Walter Scott, is that he had to write about repressed puritanical Protestant women, whereas in France, Catholic women, sinning or virtuous, offer matter for the sublime. And versions of that woman's sublime do come to you in reading Balzac: something beyond the social confines, something that opens up a space of freedom and unlimited desire for a time, while also marking the severe limits to flights of freedom.

WRITING, TALKING, DEVOURING PRESSES

The Novel in the Newspaper

Reading Balzac's immense and crucial *Lost Illusions* (*Illusions perdues*), the novel that Georg Lukács described as the "tragi-comic epic of the capitalization of spirit," in which we see the aspiring poet and novelist Lucien Chardon de Rubempré prostitute his talents to a journalism "without faith or law" that is corrupting literature, politics, and just about everything else, the reader who has patience for such things comes upon a preface to Part Three of the novel that seems to contradict everything the novel has demonstrated. The preface is a defense of the newspaper—against the legislators of the National Assembly. "Political leaders and institutions vanish before the writer who makes himself the voice of his time."[1] And what once bore the name of Tacitus, Luther, Calvin, or Voltaire, Rousseau, Chateaubriand, Benjamin Constant, "now is named the NEWSPAPER." In his peroration Balzac notes that the legislators of the Assembly are the "direct product" of Jean-Jacques Rousseau's *Social Contract* and *Emile,* "burned by the hand of the executioner by order of the Parlement de Paris."[2] The pen is mightier than the sword, Balzac is saying—but more than that: the very structure of constitutional rule rests on writings once banned, and the Assembly's debate upon censorship should keep that in mind.

What has set Balzac off—this provides an interesting optic for rereading *Lost Illusions*—is a debate that took place in the Assembly in June 1843, provoked by the Baron de Chapuys-Montlaville, a moderately conservative *député* from the Dauphiné and an aspiring historian, author of a local history of his region. He was proposing a new form of censorship of the novel published in serial installments in the daily newspaper. This was a very new phenomenon—the first serial novel or *roman-feuilleton* in France, appearing on page one of *La Presse* in 1836, was Balzac's *The Old Maid (La Vieille fille)*. And shortly before Chapuys-Montlaville set out on his quest, Balzac's *The Local Muse (La Muse du département)* had run in the newspaper *Le Messager* across April and May. It's a novel centered on the provincial woman writer Dinah de la Baudraye (who has some traits of George Sand), who falls in love with the cynical and corrupted Parisian journalist Etienne Lousteau, the very one who initiates Lucien de Rubempré into journalism: material bound to displease Chapuys-Montlaville. But the honorable *député*'s objections aren't aimed at the content of any one novel but at the very idea of the novel published in the newspaper. The *roman-feuilleton*, almost always printed on the bottom third or fourth of the front page—the *rez-de-chaussée* or ground floor, it was called—was gaining traction in France. In 1842 and 1843, Eugène Sue's immensely popular *The Mysteries of Paris (Les mystères de Paris)* ran for some thirteen months in the *Journal des Débats*, and in fact rescued that staid newspaper from bankruptcy. The daily dose of fiction in the paper enabled publishers to cut subscription prices by three quarters (there weren't any single-issue sales at the time), reach a much wider audience, and make up for lost revenue by paid advertising. A vast new commercial undertaking that was succeeding.

Chapuys-Montlaville believes that newspapers should stick to political news: "Illusion is the enemy of truth," he claims, though it must be said that most newspapers of the time were enlisted with one political party or another so their news was scarcely objective.[3] His proposal: that newspapers that published fiction be subjected to a tax from which newspapers that remained faithful to strictly political news be exempt. An interesting way to exercise control of the press—in a political climate where the freedom or censorship of the press was a much-debated topic. The Restoration had waffled on how much freedom to give the press, and it collapsed in the July Revolution of 1830 in good part because of its attempt to impose a draconian prior restraint, *censure préalable*, on newspapers: journalists and printers were in the vanguard during that three-day insurrection that sent the last of the Bourbon kings into exile. By the time Chapuys-Montlaville rose to speak in the Assembly, the topic was an old one, yet never fully resolved.

What Chapuys-Montlaville contributes to the debate is the traditional notion that novels are bad for you, a complaint of churchmen and moralists and censors across the ages. They are bad for you since life depicted in fiction will always be more attractive and seductive than the real thing. More precisely, novels teach people to be unhappy with their lot in life. They teach modest men "to despise the social status of their fathers and to be ashamed of their origins; they falsify in this way the simplest and, alas, the least widely accepted definition of equality."[4] In a later speech, the representative goes further: "The habitual reading of novels, by souring each citizen on his situation, as I mentioned, and by making him conceive chimerical hopes for his future, provokes *déclassement*, upsetting the place where each should find his personal dignity."[5] So there you have it: novels are agents of social discontent, promoting chimerical notions of social ascension, changing places, instead of remaining in your assigned place in the social hierarchy. A typical complaint of the social conservative—one to which Balzac ostensibly is sympathetic, except that all the energies of his novels point in the other direction, toward ambition and social change. The French Revolution unleashed personal ambition, and then Napoleon's ideal of "career open to talent" (*la carrière ouverte au talent*) made the ambitious young man—and occasional woman, such as the heroine of *The Provincial Muse*—the typical protagonist of the French novel, from Stendhal to Balzac and beyond. Chapuys-Montlaville's description of what he sees as typical readers of novels fits the bill: they are "anxious, frivolous, ambitious minds that throw themselves, without reflection, without a true vocation, into the hazards of great cities, where too often they encounter misery and shame." That's a pretty accurate description of Lucien's Paris career. And that's the matter that Balzac loves.

One more line from the honorable representative: he notes that it is "disagreeable to live in the upper storey of a house whose ground floor is '*aussi mal habité*'": inhabited by social undesirables. He alludes of course to the ground floor of the newspaper, inhabited by the serial novel. Sheer snobbism, of the type you find a few years earlier in the contemporary critic C. A. Sainte-Beuve's essay "On Industrial Literature," which laments the coming of the serial novel and the popular novel as marking the decline of standards and the loss of "good writing." He deplores the democratization of literature that is closely tied to the rise of the newspaper. Balzac does so as well, and the very journalists of *Lost Illusions* speak for him in describing organs that pander to the worst instincts of the public. But where Sainte-Beuve draws back snobbishly from the phenomenon, Balzac plunges in. *Lost Illusions* thrives on the dramas created by the industrialization of literary production.

Lucien comes to Paris with two manuscripts in his baggage: a volume of sonnets called *The Daisies (Les Marguerites)* and a novel entitled *The Soldier of Charles IX (L'Archer de Charles IX)*. He tries to peddle them to the publishers/booksellers headquartered in the *Galeries de Bois*, in wooden shacks knocked up in the open space of the Palais-Royal. It is, tellingly, the center of Paris prostitution as well as publishing and book selling. *The Daisies* are a complete non-starter; they will be bought by the publisher Dauriat only after Lucien has made a name for himself in journalism; and at that point Dauriat admits to not having read them—he is buying a name, not a book. The novel has a more complex career. It's an historical novel in the manner of Walter Scott, set during the sixteenth-century Wars of Religion, a time of conflict, betrayal, savagery, and martyrdom that appealed to historians and novelists. Lucien finds no takers for it, either. His new-found literary friend Daniel d'Arthez, who represents selfless dedication to literature amidst poverty, cold, and hunger, undertakes to correct it, and turns it into what will later be considered a "masterpiece." Lucien eventually sells it to a new publishing house, Fendant et Cavalier, who are speculators in literature. Theirs is a highly leveraged operation—deeply in debt for paper, ink, and printing, they seek to publish a blockbuster that will bring in the needed capital. They pay Lucien in *lettres de change*, bills of exchange payable in three, six, and twelve months. When Lucien attempts to negotiate the *lettres de change* he finds that the publisher's credit is so shaky that he would lose fifty percent of the bills' face value. And soon enough Fendant et Cavalier go bankrupt, and Lucien's novel is remaindered at fire sale prices. Only later, after Lucien has renounced literature, and then after his death, does the novel reappear, now with a preface by d'Arthez, to become a star in the literary firmament.

Journalists Against Journalism

The critique of journalism runs throughout *Lost Illusions*, but it's at its most explicit at a post-theater party where Lucien, who has written his first drama review in an innovative style, becomes a member of the profession. Talk turns to journalism, sparked by the remark of a German diplomat that when the victorious Prussian officers, after the defeat of Napoleon, looked down at Paris from the heights of Montmartre, General Blücher responded to his comrade-in-arms Saaken, who proposed to burn Paris. "Don't you dare. France will only be destroyed by *that*"—meaning the intelligentsia gathered in the great city.[6] If they undertake to enlighten the mass of the people, that will sow revolt, the defeat of legitimate rule, the destruction of the very principle of authority. The journalist Claude Vignon agrees: newspapers are an evil, though one the government could make use of if it hadn't instead decided to fight it. Emile Blondet, another journalist, calls newspapers "poison shops," and Vignon piles on:

> The newspaper, instead of being a sacred mission, has become an arm for the political parties; and from that it's become a commercial enterprise; and like all commercial enterprises it knows neither faith nor law. Every newspaper, as Blondet puts it, is a shop where

one sells to the public words of whatever color it likes....all newspapers will in due course be cowardly, hypocritical shameless,
mendacious, murderous; they will kill ideas, systems, men, and
will thrive from doing so.   (P 5:404/ML 320)

Vignon, working himself into a tirade, goes on to say:

> We all know, such as we are, that newspapers will go farther than
> kings in ingratitude, farther than the dirtiest business dealings in
> speculations and calculations, that they will devour our brains
> every morning to sell their intellectual narcotics; but we will all
> write for them, like workers in a quicksilver mine who know that
> they will die from their labor.   (P 5:406/ML 322–3)

The exploitation of intelligence in journalism is fatal to its work-
ers—but they are condemned to this labor.

Lousteau declares of his new publication: "The newspaper
holds to be true whatever is probable. We start from that." (P 5:437/
ML 357) We are at the origin of fake news in Balzac's view. The
ferocious attack on newspapers and journalism launched by his
fictional journalists speaks to many of Balzac's obsessions.
Newspapers appeared to incarnate the very anti-principle of the
kind of political and social authority he wanted to believe in, and
clamed to think necessary for his country. There's a moment in
another Balzac novel, The Fatal Skin (La Peau de chagrin) when the
protagonist, Raphaël, runs into three friends who, shortly after the
July Revolution, have decided to start a new journal. "Journalism,
you see, is the religion of modern societies," says one of them,
"and that's progress." Why is it progress? asks another. "Because
its popes don't have to believe, and the people don't either..."[7]
Balzac's concerns are rooted in a crucial moment in the history of
the press, of printing, and politics. France in the 1820s, when

Lost Illusions is set, saw an extraordinary burgeoning of newspapers, which were becoming a daily reality and a political force of a sort unknown during the Ancien Régime. The battle over press censorship was more or less constant; the Restoration, I noted, fell in July 1830 in good part because of its attempt to muzzle the press; and the debate continued under the next regime. When someone at the party of *Lost Illusions* remarks that journalistic excess will bring new repression, novelist Raoul Nathan replies: "Bah! What can legislation do against French intellect?" (P 5:403/ML 320).

That question isn't resolved in Balzac's novel, nor even truly in his mind. He shares his fictional journalists' estimate of the excesses of journalism; his belief in legitimacy makes him deplore the power of the press. And yet he is caught up in its dynamism. He was himself both novelist and journalist, as were so many writers at the time: the press of all sorts was their outlet and their crucial ally in publicizing their books. Some of his rage against publishers and editors is that of the exploited against the exploiters. This would take a particularly acute form when he sued the publisher François Buloz, editor of *La Revue de Paris* (of the *Revue des Deux-Mondes* also) when he sold uncorrected proofs of Balzac's *Lily of the Valley* (*Le lys dans la vallée*) for publication in a French language Russian periodical, showing a high disregard for Balzac's intellectual property and his dedication to thorough revision of his work. But Balzac's objections to what the press has become go deeper; they are more profound than the critique offered by the conservative *député*.

We get an enactment of the problem when Lucien, now a regular on the journal edited by Lousteau, is tasked with writing articles first for, then against, then in the middle on Raoul Nathan's new novel. The newspaper decides it needs to attack Nathan, and Lucien is chosen to lead the assault. When Lucien protests that he considers Nathan's novel a masterpiece and has nothing to say against it, Lousteau chastises him:

> "Hah! My dear boy, learn your trade," Lousteau replied with a laugh. "Even if it's a masterpiece, under your pen it must become a stupid piece of trash, a dangerous and unhealthy work."
> "But how?"
> "You'll change its beauties into flaws."
> "I'm incapable of such a tour de force."
> "My dear, a journalist is an acrobat…"   (P 5:442/ML 363)

Lousteau explains how it's done: by making the novel representative of a tendency unhealthy to French letters. Lucien produces a persuasive critique that both pleases the journal and furthers his career: Dauriat, Nathan's publisher, comes to offer him a contract for *The Daisies*. But not long after his editors decide that it's time to rehabilitate Nathan: they need his good offices. So Lucien now must write in praise of the novel. When he protests he now has nothing good to say of it, his colleagues pile on:

> "You actually believed what you wrote? Hector asked Lucien.
> "Yes."
> "My boy," said Blondet, "I thought you smarter than that!"
> (P:457/ML 380)

Blondet then goes on to offer a new lesson to Lucien: everything is bilateral in the domain of thought. "Ideas are binary. Janus is the god of criticism and the symbol of genius." Vernou adds: "You believed in what you wrote?…But we are salesmen of sentences, and we live off that commerce." Blondet proceeds to explain how to manage the rehabilitation of Nathan's book—and ends by proposing that the following weekend Lucien write a third article (this alone will be signed with his name) in which he reconciles the two earlier critiques as part of a debate provoked by all important works of literature. Lucien now gets it, and he goes to work counseled by his mistress, the actress Coralie, who says: "Don't I go on this evening dressed as an Andalusian, tomorrow as a gypsy, and another day cross-dressed as a man? Do like me, give them disguises for their money, and let's live happily." (P 5:461/ML 385)

The analogy of writing to acting is disquieting. It suggests that all that matters is the illusion one produces. And here I think we cut to the quick of Balzac's critique of journalism and its role in the modernity he rejects: the journalistic word has ceased to have any connection with the reality that it is supposed to represent. It has become a kind of empty signifier that can be made to say anything, to mean anything. There is a deep analogy to money. If language is often analogized to money in the work of the great linguist Ferdinand de Saussure it's because they are both, in his eyes, arbitrary systems of equivalence and exchange. For Balzac that's a problem. He is nostalgic for a time when wealth was essentially tied to land, to what we think of as real property. Now it seems to be simply the speculative creation of Nucingen and his ilk. Likewise language ought to be rooted in its natural referents, in its expressive potential, as a kind of natural or God-given human power. He subscribes, I think, to Romantic theories of language that see it derived from natural facts, as in Johann Gottfried Herder's essay on the origins of language, as in Ralph Waldo Emerson's essay "Nature." If language can be used in the way that Lousteau, Blondet, and Lucien use it, to manipulate and simulate meaning, then we are in for a world of trouble. Trouble in the very system of communication and representation that Balzac uses.

Words, Money, Signs

As we will note in the opening pages of *Sarrasine*, where the origin of the Lanty family wealth is under discussion, when you can't pin wealth to land holding, you are in a troubled sign system: not only doesn't money smell, its origins are unclear, often untraceable and unknowable. Categories break down. At the end of *Sarrasine,* in Roland Barthes' analysis, the discovery that the painter Sarrasine's beloved Zambinella isn't a woman at all but a castrato lifts the bar of repression over the truth, but also the bar of sexual categorization, male or female, creating a kind of "pandemic of signs," the breakdown of gender classifications that perhaps underlie all others.[8] The same may be true for money: when you lose the sense of its origins, it circulates without foundation and without restraint, creating bubbles of inflation and moments of crash that are both familiar to most of Balzac's young heroes. It's a boom or bust economy of signs in general. Money is perhaps merely the most obvious face of a sign system that is overall in trouble. Rastignac, Lucien, and others such as Raphaël de Valentin and Victurnien d'Esgrignon and many more have to learn to read the signs of society and of the city. Their initiation into Paris is largely a reading lesson: how to see what is hidden under social appearances, how to detect what wealth underpins—or not—social status, who is sexually and financially involved with whom. There are many passages about reading the cityscape—a notable one comes at the start of *Ferragus* (one of the three novellas of *Story of the*

Thirteen [*Histoire des Treize*]), where the narrator describes the moral qualifications of different streets in Paris: those that are young, or old, respectable or dishonored, or noble, or murderous, and so on. Each street has its "physiognomy" that imprints certain ideas on the observer.[9] Just as the lodgers in the Pension Vauquer, in *Père Goriot*, suggest "dramas, past or in action" and raise questions: "What acid had stripped her of her feminine forms? She must have been pretty and well put together: was it vice, sorrow, greed? Had she loved too much?…" (P 3:57/S 14). And so on. Balzac believed in the pseudo-science of physiognomy: it contributed to his semiotic enterprise, reading the signs of the city and the social distinctions of modern life. Another tale from *Story of the Thirteen*, *The Girl with the Golden Eyes*, begins with a physiognomy of the Parisian crowd, always hurried, harried, fatigued, driven by two forces: "gold and pleasure."

Sign systems are enormously important in Balzac's novels. In the bourgeois nineteenth century, older signs of social distinction have been lost. In the Ancien Régime—at least in Balzac's nostalgic view—you could tell who someone was from his or her appearance, from clothing first of all and then manner, comportment. In the nineteenth century, the men all wear black and carry top hats, untrue for the proletariat of course but it's mainly the upwardly mobile bourgeois and the various levels of aristocracy that interest Balzac. And even bourgeois women can learn to be fashionable, to display the signs of social belonging, to be *"comme il faut,"* though the truly penetrating observer will be able to detect the difference between that and true nobility. Distinction—creating one's own distinctive style, detecting social distinction in others—becomes a crucial process. When Lucien de Rubempré arrives in Paris from provincial Angoulême, he goes for a walk in the Tuileries Garden:

"two cruel hours" that teach him how unfashionable his clothing is, how deficient his whole appearance. In particular, he discovers "the world of necessary superfluities." (P 5:270/ML 169) These are detailed:

> He noticed ravishing studs on shirts whose whiteness made his own look yellowed in comparison! All these elegant gentlemen wore the most marvelous gloves, while his were only fit for a police-man. One toyed with an exquisitely mounted cane; another wore a shirt with delicious gold cuff-links. One, as he chatted with a woman, twisted an elegant riding crop. There were a few splashes of mud on the full pleats of his breeches, and from his clicking spurs and his tight-fitting jacket it was evident that he was about to remount one of the two horses held by a diminutive groom, a *tiger*. Another drew from his waistcoat pocket a watch thin as a five-franc piece, and glanced at the time with the air of a man who is either too early or too late for a rendezvous. As he looked at these pretty trifles whose very existence he had never suspected, the world of necessary superfluities appeared before him, and he shud-dered to think what an enormous capital was needed to exercise the part of the elegant young man.

The narrator admonishes us, a page earlier, not to consider the experience of Lucien in the Tuileries puerile: the question of cos-tume is "enormous for those who wish to appear to have what they don't have, since it is often the best way to possess it later." (P 5:269/ML 169) Small things can torment brilliant lives.

I see Balzac here calling attention to and providing an apologia for his attention to detail. That's one of his claims to be an observer and recorder of his time but it's also the very basis of his semiotic enterprise. Those necessary superfluities demand our attention because in the modern world, where the traditional signs have become blurred, they tell us who people are. Lucien's beauty cannot be detected without proper clothing and accessorizing.

His emergence into Parisian fashion passes through phases: his first attempt to improve his appearance through a quick purchase of ready-made clothing results in his looking, during his evening at the Opéra with his former protectress from Angoulême, Louise de Bargeton, and her fashionable Parisian cousin the Marquise d'Espard, like "a shop boy in his Sunday best," in the words of the Marquise (P 5:284/ML 184). It will only be later, after his first success as a journalist and as the lover of the fashion-savvy Coralie, who spends extravagantly to deck out her man, that Lucien acquires "the elegant furnishings of the elegant that he had so desired during his first walk in the Tuileries. Lucien now had marvelous canes, a charming lorgnette, diamond studs, rings for his morning cravats, signet rings, and waistcoats magnificent to behold, in a variety of colors to match his costume." (P 5:479/ML 405) He finally appears as what he wants to be. We may be reminded of the tailor summoned by Rastignac in *Père Goriot* who considers himself a "hyphen" between a young man's present and future (P 3:130/S 102). When Lucien gets himself fitted out by Staub, that fashionable men's tailor tells him: "A young man dressed as you are can go stroll in the Tuileries, he will marry a rich Englishwoman within two weeks." (P 5:289/ML 190) Appearance will create reality. It will produce the money needed to support appearance.

As Balzac's narrator recognizes, this all may appear a bit childish, and certainly there are many readers over the years who have rejected Balzac because of his attachment to the seemingly trivial detail and to the values of the marketplace. There is to be sure a certain vulgarity to his catalogues of possessions and things. He produces what can appear a self-parody in his "Inventory of the rue Fortunée," the inventory he prepared of all the furniture and accessories in the house he bought to receive his bride, Evelina Hanska, following their marriage in the Ukraine in 1850—the house he enjoyed only for a short time since he died soon after his return to Paris. He moves through the house room by room, detailing everything in each room, putting a price tag on everything. It appears the realized dream of an ambitious parvenu, and Balzac can be considered such. But as with his flamboyantly reactionary political positions that in themselves may appear offensive, there is an analytic reward for his materialist obsessions. His reaction against the politics of his moment allows him to see the contradictions and corruptions of contemporary France with an acuteness that was, as I mentioned, applauded by Marx and Engels. His manic concern with objects, furniture, accessories, and their market price allows him to grasp the semiotics of social distinction. And that makes him the best contemporary analyst of the world in which he is immersed. As the historian Pierre Rosanvallon has noted, before the invention of sociology (which would come soon, in the seminal work of Auguste Comte), it was novelists who furnished the "principles of intelligibility" for the understanding of society.[10] And no other novelist quite so much as Balzac, whose readings of the society of his time, its geographies and topographies, its houses and possessions, remain a principal source for those seeking to understand the forces at work in early nineteenth century France.[11] Balzac's immersion in the values of the marketplace, his understanding of the meaning of the things people acquire to render their existence meaningful and symbolic, make him the best analyst of his time and, beyond that, a remarkable analyst of all the ways in which humans make meaning for their bare existence.

Another Study of Womankind (Autre étude de femme) contains a long discussion on the creature of fashion, the *femme comme il faut,* who has replaced the *grande dame* of the Ancien Régime. The woman of fashion has impeccable taste, she dresses with perfect appropriateness for every occasion, she always presents herself as attractive and a good conversationalist. But all the participants in this discussion agree that she is a product of a world made more bourgeois. She is a creation, not a natural product of nobility. A Russian prince joins the conversation by noting: "The death knell of high society is sounding, do you hear? ... And the first toll is that modern expression of yours, 'the creature of fashion.'"[12] The extended conversational analysis of this creature of fashion notes all the signs that she deploys, that she knows how to use in her self-fashioning, and that those persons she meets equally know how to decipher. It's a curious discussion in that the *femme comme il faut* is clearly an attractive, even seductive creature yet equally clearly not a *grande dame* in the manner of the pre-Revolutionary noblewoman who did not have to think of her dress or manner, who was instinctively the product of her caste, with the nonchalance that comes only with high, unreflective, and unanalyzed social position. I think it's fair to say that in Balzac's understanding the French Revolution created the modern world of signs—before the Revolution there was no need for semiotic analysis since signs were fixed and unproblematic. Sign-systems, including money and class, are products of the vertiginously unanchored modern world. And that must be true of language as well. The writer, like Lucien, is something of an acrobat, creating meaning (perhaps only ephemerally) through words rather than reflecting established truths.

Digesting and Talking

Another Study of Womankind takes place in the small drawing room of Félicité des Touches' townhouse, at a select late supper party that follows her larger party, her *rout,* a word and a custom taken over from the English. English inventions, says the narrator, are currently *"mecanifying"* other nations, making their social life as boring as that in England. The "rout" is one more sign of a falling away from the sociable customs of the Ancien Régime. The after-party hosted by Félicité des Touches (who is a well-known novelist under the pen name Camille Maupin) is "thus, in France, in a few houses, a welcome affirmation of the spirit that was once ours in this ebullient land."(P 3:674/NY 18). It affirms an earlier order where everyone understands without explanation, everyone is witty and makes a contribution to the general conversation. But there are good reasons that such late suppers have become rare in France of the 1830s:

> It is because there have never been, under any regime, fewer people settled, established, and secure than under the reign of Louis-Philippe, in which the Revolution has begun a second time, legally. Everyone strives toward some goal or scurries after fortune. Time has become the dearest commodity on the market, and so no one can indulge in the prodigious prodigality of returning home the next morning and sleeping late.   (P 3:674/NY 18)

So the conversation in Félicité des Touches' salon is consciously an echo of the Ancien Régime. It offers a kind of authenticity of friendship and social exchange that appears to stand in contrast to the world of inflated and deceptive signs in which Lucien works.

The narrator prepares us for his report of this particular evening:

Ingenious repartee, subtle observations, sparkling gibes, pictures painted with brilliant clarity came thick and fast in a spontaneous, effervescent rush, offered up without arrogance or artifice, spoken with sincerity, and savored with delight.... Secrets artfully betrayed, exchanges both light and deep, everything undulates, spins, changes luster and color with each passing sentence. Keen judgments and breathless narrations follow one upon the next. Every eye listens, every gesture is a question, every glance an answer.   (P 3:675/NY 19)

The conversation this evening turns to storytelling: we will have a set of tales told by various participants, in a grand display of the "*phénomène oral*," the speech phenomenon, which will cast a magic spell.

Everything in this presentation of the reciprocal tale-telling of *Another Study of Womankind* indicates that Balzac wants to find in the oral tale something more authentic than journalism or even the novel in its industrial transformation. A number of writers throughout the nineteenth century display a nostalgia for oral storytelling: such as Guy de Maupassant and Barbey d'Aurevilly regularly frame their tales in a situation of oral telling and listening, as do Saki (H. H. Monroe) and Rudyard Kipling and Joseph Conrad, even on occasion Henry James. Walter Benjamin has given the most probing analysis of this phenomenon in his essay "The Storyteller," ostensibly devoted to Nikolai Leskov but more generally about the replacement of the oral tale, characterized by the passing on of "wisdom" from teller to listener, by the novel, the realm of the uncounseled solitary individual.[13] The storyteller speaks from a lived situation, in the workplace, or as a traveler returned from elsewhere. His tale is a hand-made object (*ein Handwerk*), the product of patient artisanal skill. All that is dying out, according to Benjamin, in a world where there is no longer patience and a sense of eternity.

In choosing Leskov as his subject, Benjamin is talking about a sophisticated later simulation of the oral, like what you have in Balzac and other writers I mentioned. Balzac's novels and tales—there are many that simulate oral exchange—coincide with the moment when European oral culture was in fact dying out. The great collections of *Kinder-und Hausmärchen* by the Grimm Brothers were published from 1812 to 1857. They captured the oral tradition as it was disappearing, preserving it in print. Balzac is of course wholly aware that he is engaged in a similar process: passing on a holdover from pre-Revolutionary oral sociability that no longer exists except in his written and printed record of it. That is the paradox that lies at the heart of *Another Study of Womankind*. Balzac wants to make us believe, through the medium of print, that we are witness to—that we are hearing, at least in a simulation—a kind of talk and a kind of storytelling that are prelapsarian, even though we have to read them.

At least as important as the stories told in *Another Story of Womankind* are the reactions noted by the listeners to them. Henri de Marsay's story of betrayal at age seventeen by his first love leads mainly to uncomfortable reactions from the women present, and then at the end—when de Marsay describes how he has emerged from the experience a cool-headed master of relationships and a future statesman—Delphine de Nucingen can't help remarking: "How I pity the second woman! (P 3:688/NY 32). This produces an "imperceptible smile" on de Marsay's lips that in turn makes Delphine blush: in fact, she realizes, as we realize, and maybe the others of the group as well, that *she* was the second woman. And we know from *Père Goriot* something about her sufferings in that role. General Armand de Montriveau tells a grim story from Napoleon's disastrous Russian campaign, about a captain whose wife has become mistress of his colonel, an arrangement that seems settled until the colonel too conspicuously reveals it to other officers gathered in their farmhouse bivouac. In the morning, the captain sets fire to the farmhouse; we hear his wife's screams as the house is engulfed in flames. De Marsay's comment on the story draws its moral: "There is nothing so fearsome as the revolt of a sheep." (P 3:709/NY 53) Madame de Portenduère objects that the story will give her nightmares, and that it shouldn't be the last impression left by the evening. Whereupon Horace Bianchon, the doctor who tends to so many patients across *The Human Comedy*, offers a final tale, that of "la Grande Bretèche," the name of a property that was the scene of a horrific vengeance. It's a complex tale that Bianchon has to wheedle from a chambermaid who is the one remaining witness to the event. In brief: when a husband discovers his wife's affair with a Spanish nobleman, he makes her swear that she is alone in her bedroom—and when she does, he proceeds to summon a mason to wall up the closet in which her lover in fact is hiding. He spends the next twenty days in her bedroom, until there are no more sounds from the closet. "You swore," he says to her, "that there was no one there…"

This fierce tale of vengeance ends the evening. There is nothing left to say. The women rise from the supper table, breaking the spell left by Bianchon's narration. Some of them, we are told, feel a shiver from his final words. At the end of *Sarrasine*, when the narrator has finished his tale of the castrato Zambinella, his listener, the Marquise de Rochefide, turns aside from the erotic reward she implicitly promised him for telling the story she wanted to hear. "Ah! You know how to punish a man!" he says, as if registering that he as teller has been struck by the castration he has told about (P 6:1075/NY 141). The Marquise tells him to leave her. And in the last line of the novella: "The Marquise remained pensive." The tale told produces this pensivity, thought about its meanings for human relationship, for love and its consequences. That thoughtfulness represents the intended outcome of all stories told. They resonate in the lives of their listeners. They demand to be processed.

The Baron de Nucingen, Alsatian banker who speaks French with a German accent, sums up the situation of storytelling and listening in *Another Study of Womankind*: "'Ach! Vhat a bleasure to zit hier tichesting vile you talk!' said the Baron de Nucingen." (P 3:701/NY 46) This is Nucingen in uncharacteristically relaxed mode: not out rapaciously manipulating capital but made genial by storytelling. His remark sets Balzac's novella in the distinguished context of the banquet crowned with storytelling, from Plato onwards, perhaps most illustrated during the Renaissance: eating and talking in an easy harmony, to produce pleasure and enlightenment.[14] The conjunction of eating and talking in Balzac has a special resonance, since, as I earlier suggested, the relationship of his young protagonists to the world is figured as devourment, ingestion, a kind of primary orality. This in turn tends to make the reader as well into a devourer, ready to ingest ever more, ready to binge upon *The Human Comedy*'s seemingly unending offer of more to eat. The string of stories, the next picking up from the one before it, represents a particularly satisfying solution to the ever-renewed appetite for story. You come to understand that everyone in Balzac's world has a story to tell. And that means you look forward to moments when a number of them gather together to exchange stories: that's a kind of narrative utopia. One that, as the opening of *Another Study of Womankind* tells us, is disappearing. It remains as a nostalgic recall of the Ancien Régime.

Literature, Industry, Language

The present and the future stand rather under the iron necessity of industrialized literature. The opening paragraph of *Lost Illusions* curiously begins not with human actors or even their milieu but rather with the printing press in Angoulême: "At the moment this story begins, the Stanhope press and inking rollers weren't yet functioning in small provincial print shops." (P 5:123/ML 3) But soon we are learning about the "devouring mechanical presses" that are to come. They will of course swallow Lucien and his poetry, grind him into a journalist, toss him out when used up. The nostalgia for an earlier regime of literary composition more closely tied to the values of sociability and the exchange of ideas about life has a forceful ideal presence throughout Balzac's work, but it is joined to a consciousness that modern forces of production have made those conditions of storytelling rare. The modern writer cannot enjoy the leisure of Félicité des Touches' supper table. He has to be out there producing copy for the devouring presses, staying up all night, drinking endless cups of coffee, a worker in the quicksilver mine.

Balzac's novel about an aspiring provincial woman of letters, Dinah de la Baudraye of *The Provincial Muse,* contains an extraordinary passage that claims attention in this context. Etienne Lousteau, once Lucien's initiator into journalism, and still living a hand-to-mouth existence on his writings, has come from Paris to Sancerre, where he undertakes the seduction of Dinah. He receives a package containing proof of an article of his, wrapped in *maculatures*: that is to say, pages of printed material spoiled by ink spots, thus used as wrapping paper. Rather than attending to his own article, Lousteau starts reading to the company assembled at the

La Baudraye residence the fragmentary text of the wrapping paper, a Gothic novel from the Empire period entitled *Olympia, ou les vengeances romaines (Olympia, or Roman Vengeance).*[15] What he's got of the text begins on page 204, then jumps around to different fragments. Between declamation of the fragments, Lousteau comments on them, extrapolating characters and a plot from the meager givens. It appears to be all about vengeance, of a husband on his wife's lover, at least in Lousteau's interpretation of the plot. Balzac's fragmentary parody novel (a bit like the penny dreadfuls he wrote during his twenties) read and commented on in the context of the provincial social gathering, where most of the guests can't follow Lousteau's wit, is a vastly entertaining tour de force, a kind of mini history of the novel in Balzac's time as well as a reflection on how novels are read, taken into readers' imaginative lives. The reading also is a scene of seduction, as in Dante's tale of Paolo and Francesca ("*Galeotto fu il libro, e chi lo scrisse*") and so many others: Dinah has come alive under Lousteau's attention, and will soon become his mistress. This does not pass unperceived by her diminutive husband. In a final exchange of commentaries on the reading, Dinah notes that the Olympia of the book is happy despite threats of vengeance. No, says her husband while lighting his candle before going off to bed, because she has a lover. His words look forward to Dinah's fate as the neglected mistress of the wholly narcissistic Lousteau. He will continue to be tied up in the world of journalism, never the success as a writer he wanted to be, always somehow prisoner of those ink-stained pages. It's almost as if the physicality of the printed and misprinted page were there to spoil everything, including love. Printed words can be seductive, but that does not make them trustworthy.

What can be salvaged in language in the situation of the modern writer? Is it all a matter of that which was solid melting into air? The drama of *The Human Comedy* is played out in many registers. One of them is surely the word, the linguistic sign which has been both inflated and devalued in an overheated literary and journalistic economy. Rescuing the word from the edge of the abyss of meaninglessness is part of Balzac's enterprise. All the while that he demonstrates the encroachment of nihilism and meaninglessness he constantly insists and demonstrates that meaning is everywhere. His semiotic enterprise and his melodramatic representations both put him in the situation of Freud, for example, who liked to call himself "conquistador" because of his victories over the mute, the repressed, the seemingly unsemantic. Freud finds meaning everywhere, in our silences, our verbal lapses, our impaired movements, our faulty and incomplete stories. In my own reading, Balzac and Freud over the years have become mutually illuminating. You could say that Freud stands as a retrospective exemplum for Balzac: the kind of thought toward which Balzac seems to be headed. I was a few years ago astonished, and in some way gratified, to discover that the last book Freud read in his lifetime—before his physician gave him the lethal dose of morphine he asked for—was Balzac's *The Fatal Skin*. Two responses to the void.

In Balzac as in Freud, nothing should be left unsaid because everything is potentially full of meaning. If only you can get to it. If only you can press hard enough on the surface of things to get to what lies behind. If only you can detail and analyze with enough acuity the accessories that humans have chosen to bedeck themselves that their sign-system is made intelligible. If only you can keep up storytelling long enough for it to make a difference with its listeners. The enterprise is caught up in the logic of capitalist production and expansion. But it also has its own logic of more—filling in blanks of meaning, creating a fictional world that, in distinction to the world outside it, is fully legible.

4

THE SHAPE OF TIME

I want to return to *A Murky Business*, which I evoked earlier in its rousing story of Laurence de Cinq-Cygne, because it does something that many critics, including Henry James, warn novelists against: it stages a mixture of mainly fictional but also some "real" persons. Napoleon, Talleyrand, Fouché, Sieyès all appear, sometimes in cameo roles but always with decisive actions. There is a certain audacity to that. It rewrites official history, history known to all, from the underside, alleging the private motives of public actions. The last novel that Balzac completed before his premature death bears the title, *The Underside of History (L'Envers de l'histoire contemporaine)*.[1] It stages a kind of reverse mirror image of his powerful secret societies of supermen, such as "The Thirteen" or the convict group known as "The Grand Fanadels": it's about a secret group of do-gooders. Again and again, one might say always, Balzac addresses himself to the movement and the deep meaning of history. A famous anecdote claims that he kept a bust of Napoleon in his study, with underneath it written the boast: What he started with the sword, I will finish with the pen. Here the writing of history seems to stand on the same ground as the making of history. If Napoleon's creation of modern France remained incomplete, it was the task of the novelist to finish it, to give us all the effects and also the causes of the nation and its new dynamics.

Politics and the Novel

Maybe the best entry into Balzac's representations of modern history and the meaning of historical time would be a return to the unfinished novel that I briefly evoked earlier, about an election in a provincial town, *The Member from Arcis (Le Député d'Arcis)*. This was the novel he conceived before *A Murky Business*, then set aside for a time to fill in the background to many of the characters, who carry into the election at Arcis-sur-Aube the baggage of the past: we have here a second generation, just about thirty-five years later, that still is burdened with the story of *A Murky Business*. The novel opens with an electoral rally for Simon Giguet, nephew of the gendarme who came with Corentin and Peyrade to arrest the young Simeuse and Hauteserre in the Château de Cinq-Cygne; we encounter Malin de Gondreville, now in his nineties; Laurence de Cinq-Cygne exercises political influence from her nearby château; François Michu, son of the executed watch dog, is public prosecutor at Arcis. The election campaign of 1839 will reveal large historical movements: the rise of the bourgeoisie represented by Giguet, who has his eyes on a marriage with Cécile Beauvisage, the richest young woman of the town, seemingly the daughter of Philéas Beauvisage who made a fortune in hosiery but really the illegitimate offspring of the Vicomte de Chargeboeuf, from the younger branch of the family of the Marquis de Chargeboeuf who accompanied Laurence on her mission to Napoleon at Jena. And we witness also the alliance of former implacable enemies, the Cinq-Cygne and the Gondreville, the old nobility and the recently-minted, in an attempt to beat back the rising influence of the middle class.

The novel begins with the attempt of the ambitious Simon Giguet to put himself forward as candidate of the *juste-milieu,* those who support the middle-of-the-road policies of the "King of the French," Louis-Philippe, in a district that has up till now been represented by a "liberal," the banker François Keller, son-in-law of Comte Malin de Gondreville, that survivor from a revolutionary and Napoleonic past who has achieved the status of a *notable* and a power broker in Arcis-sur-Aube. The Château de Cinq-Cygne has now become a site of political power, one that will attempt to thwart Giguet's election: in 1839, Giguet can't hope for support from the authentic old aristocracy. The drama of Laurence and her Simeuse cousins continues to influence everything in Arcis. Giguet's Bonapartist father, Colonel Giguet, and the *notaire* Grévin bore witness against the Simeuse twins and Michu at their trial in 1805 for the kidnapping of Gondreville. They despoiled the Simeuse of their fortune, which their Hauteserre uncle and Laurence only gradually restored. In the first years of the Restoration, Gondreville managed to preserve his occult power by means of Grévin, Colonel Giguet, his son-in-law Keller—repeatedly reelected as député—and influence at the court of Louis XVIII, but that ceases in 1824 when Louis dies and is replaced by the reactionary Charles X, which allows Laurence to name Michu's lawyer son as chief judge in Arcis in compensation for his father's victimization by the liberals and Bonapartists. It's all very complicated for the reader, in fact largely incomprehensible unless you know the complex plots and counter-plots of *A Murky Business.*

The election does not take place on a fresh slate; everything at stake is under the weight of the past. The very electoral machinations that the novel recounts seem to represent a present that is fallen and sordid in comparison to the heroic and tragic story of the Simeuse, Hauteserre, Michu, and especially Laurence de Cinq-Cygne.

Now comes the news that Charles Keller, son of the current député and slated to be his successor, has been killed fighting in Algeria, the recently acquired colony that the French army was "pacifying." This leaves the liberals at a loss, and appears to open the way to Giguet, whose electoral success would allow him to make the advantageous marriage to Cécile Beauvisage, and claim the biggest house in town. But wait. With the death of Charles Keller, powerful interests decide there must be a new candidate to oppose Giguet. Not only are some local *notables*, including the *sous-préfet*, making counter-schemes, there is a more powerful machination underway in Paris, at the hôtel of the Marquise d'Espard, no less. We know her from many another novel, especially *Lost Illusions* where she becomes the implacable enemy to Lucien de Rubempré. Now her circle makes the choice of a man who will travel incognito to Arcis-sur-Aube, negotiate with both the Gondreville and the Cinq-Cygne, and quickly become the immediate focus of attention and gossip, as well as of Cécile's matrimonial ambitions.

The *inconnu* who has come to Arcis turns out to be Maxime de Trailles, all too well known from other volumes of *The Human Comedy*: the former lover of Anastasie de Restaud, a Goriot daughter whom he manipulates and bankrupts, a member of The Thirteen, a largely sinister figure described at one point as "a brilliant ring linking Parisian society to the underworld."[2] Maxime wants to "*faire une fin*," bring a decent dénouement to his thus far disreputable life: what could be better than elected office? It's Eugène de Rastignac, now at the height of his political power, who gives him his electoral instructions, noting that his rival Giguet is motivated by Cécile's dowry, which Maxime might well seek for himself—marriage to a daughter of a provincial industrialist is the best he can hope for since his vices are too well known in Paris. So along with advice to cultivate the Cinq-Cygne for Legitimist votes, and 25,000 francs in cash, Maxime jumps into his tilbury and heads to Arcis.

Election in Balzac reflects and represents the power nuances of different social strata in the provinces in 1839. But it also turns on the most traditional of Balzacian concerns: how to finance your ambitions. As Thomas Piketty argued in *Capital in the Twenty-first Century*, the best way to accede to fortune has long been through marriage to capital.[3] The dowry is a major player in Balzac's narratives. Grévin, whose granddaughter Cécile was to marry Charles Keller, now would prefer to arrange a marriage with a descendant of Laurence de Cinq-Cygne, but suspects that's impossible because of his past alliance with Gondreville. Giguet wants Cécile's dowry, and it seems Maxime de Trailles does too: he needs the money, and his backers need to keep the upstarts like Giguet from assuming power. Politics converges with traditional interests of local dynasties, alliances, and allegiances, and the acquisition of property. The scheming and sharp elbowing of politics differ little from the dramas of ambition played out in *Père Goriot* and *Lost Illusions* and many another novel. It's social climbing by other means.

And while this novel begins with the ascension of Simon Giguet as typical representative of the emergent bourgeoisie that more and more dominates in the July Monarchy, the weight of the past on the election in Arcis suggests that Balzac's emotional allegiance really goes to the Legitimists, and especially to the Cinq-Cygne clan. Laurence de Cinq-Cygne is of course one of his most striking women characters, one who dominates through her willpower, whose eros was so powerful that it seemingly required two men, the Simeuse twins, to match it, who never accepted the new order in France yet made a kind of separate and personal peace with Napoleon because she recognized him as a man of destiny on a par with herself, and who lives on in the family château as a kind of rule unto herself. Laurence represents the best Legitimacy has to offer, a personal myth that Balzac cannot divest himself of even when dealing with an election nine years into the reign of Louis-Philippe. The Giguet candidacy, on the other hand, allows him to approach something like the Flaubertian *sottisier,* or "dictionary of received ideas," in the enumeration of the clichés of bourgeois progressivism: "They declared themselves for railroads, mackintoshes, penitentiaries, wooden road paving, the independence of negroes, savings banks, shoes without seams, gas streetlamps, paved sidewalks, universal voting rights, the reduction of the civil list" ("*On se déclarait ainsi pour les chemins de fer, les mackintosh, les pénitenciers, le pavage en bois, l'indépendance des nègres, les caisses d'épargne, les souliers sans couture, l'éclairage au gaz, les trottoirs en asphalte, le vote universel, la réduction de la liste civile.*")[4] That's good. But it doesn't give any hope for the electoral idea. Balzac doesn't really believe in the commonwealth.

It's interesting that Stendhal also wrote a novel, half a novel really, devoted to an election in the same period (1834 as opposed to Balzac's 1839), and that it also remains unfinished. The second volume of his *Lucien Leuwen* is all about an election in a provincial town. Lucien, a young employee of the Ministry of the Interior, is sent to Normandy as *commissaire aux élections,* that is someone charged with making sure that the electoral results are favorable to the government. He is armed with the usual weaponry of July Monarchy elections: positions to distribute, including tobacco concessions; positions to take away, as in the sacking of postal clerks; the promise of new roads leading to the estates of local *notables,* and cash. In the town of Caen he faces his biggest electoral challenge: to defeat by any and all means M. Mairobert, a local notable who is respected and honest but independent in his ways. He says to his assistant, Coffe: "The Minister told me he'd spend 500,000 francs not to have Mairobert facing him in the Chamber. Weigh that carefully: money now says everything."[5] The local *préfet,* who is, like all *préfets,* charged with producing electoral results favorable to the government, has backed a loser against Mairobert. So Lucien comes up with a somewhat desperate counter-scheme: to back the Legitimist candidate, who would be less thorny in the Chamber than Mairobert, and swing supporters of the government-backed candidate to him. He visits the local clergy and Legitimist nobility with a promise of 100,000 francs if they can gather the needed votes from the country gentlemen in the region. Lucien's plan doesn't quite succeed— Mairobert wins despite his efforts. But curiously, despite his and Stendhal's cynicism about the electoral process, the moment the electoral college assembles in Caen, and his efforts to influence the outcome are at an end, Lucien comments, with what I think is genuine admiration: "There's the people truly sovereign" ("*Voilà le people vraiment souverain*"). And Coffe remarks: "You'll see, after thirty or forty years of elections, the provincial Frenchman will be less stupid." The election of 1834 was famously corrupt: not a single republican candidate was allowed to win. But there may be a redeeming feature in the electoral principle: a future reduction of stupidity.

Not so for Balzac. If Stendhal's election looks toward a possibly redemptive future, Balzac's seems to be all about the dead weight of the past. You can't explain the present without it. This is true for what you might call dynastic reasons—how the house of Cinq-Cygne has interacted with that of Gondreville, for instance—but also because French history writ large weighs on his characters so heavily. You can't understand or situate a Simon Giguet or a François Keller without referring back at least as far as the French Revolution, and then the whole of its sequel: the rise of Napoleon, the Napoleonic wars, the coming of the Bourbon Restoration, the collapse of the Restoration in the July Revolution of 1830 and the arrival on the throne of the "citizen king" Louis-Philippe. It seems that Balzac can't get on with his election novel because each present political issue, each choice to be made about the future, inevitably leads back into the past, into questions of where and how the issues arose and developed. It is curious that neither *The Member from Arcis* nor *Lucien Leuwen* managed to get finished. In Stendhal's case, that seems a matter of the plot, which Stendhal always had trouble managing unless he had a template, a pre-existing story that told him how it must end (the case for *The Red and the Black* and *The Charterhouse of Parma*). For Balzac, it may rather be part of a dynamic that powers the whole of *The Human Comedy*: the need to connect all the dots, to show how everything is caused by something else, to make all the parts explain one another, to attempt to say everything that needs to be said about men and women in history.

There would be many ways to follow up on this assertion. One would be to look at political careers in *The Human Comedy*. I touched on Malin de Gondreville's in passing: grandson of a stonemason in Troyes, he goes to Paris with a letter of recommendation to Danton, gets elected to the Convention Nationale (the revolutionary legislature) in 1793, at the time of the Terror, but remains wisely in the shadows until Thermidor overthrows the Jacobins, and then gets on splendidly. He marries the daughter of someone who has made millions in supplying the army, he buys the Gondreville estate in 1800 under cover of his agent, gets appointed to the Conseil d'Etat by the First Consul, Napoleon; is elected Senator in 1809; plays a double (or triple) game between Napoleon and the Bourbons; becomes a favorite of King Louis XVIII following the Restoration, then a courtier under Louis-Philippe—a slippery servant of all regimes. His career is not atypical of a period of continuing upheaval with lots of opportunity for political advancement, and betrayal. The case of Henri de Marsay, whom we come to know more intimately, is more difficult to understand. He appears at first, and repeatedly, as an insouciant young dandy whose appeal to women explains his social standing, although he treats them wretchedly. He marries a rich Englishwoman, daughter of a brewer, and before we know it we find him prime minister and a highly reputed statesman. His large experience of women, he implies, has turned him into a polished and self-contained political figure. Sometimes that appears to be his only qualification for high office, though he has also participated in various schemes of The Thirteen, that mysterious band of supermen devoted to one another. Then there is Eugène de Rastignac, whose social advancement we know more about, especially in his passive alliance with his mistress's husband's banking schemes: Nucingen makes Rastignac's fortune for him, and eventually he marries (this is a bit shocking) his mistress' daughter, Augusta de Nucingen. So his arrival at money and social prominence is explained, but we're never quite sure how he moves from that to political power. He becomes under-secretary of State in de Marsay's government, then minister of Justice. As for Maxime de Trailles whom we see at the very end of what was completed of *The Member from Arcis*, his past career would seem to be heading him to prison rather than the summits of political power. Had the novel been finished, he would no doubt have won the election and taken his seat in the Assembly. Balzac was surely aware of the decadence that implied: elections in his view are without probity.

The sense of history—political history, the history of manners and ideas—permeates Balzac's representations of people, places, actions. As Erich Auerbach writes about Balzac (and Stendhal) in *Mimesis*, representation is itself indissociable from historical process.[6] Every time a new character comes on stage—even a relatively minor one—we learn of his or her personal history in relation to the history of the nation and its conflicts between authority and contestation, between legitimacy and usurpation. Places are described in terms of their historical development, their thriving or stagnation in the emerging capitalist economy. Actions summon up historical forces as they unfold. As Georg Lukács claimed, even apparent coincidences in Balzac's plots usually reveal something profound about the dynamics and contradictions of the society he portrays. While Balzac deplored the evolution of modern French history, it gave him an enormous advantage as a novelist: the upheavals from 1789 to the time he wrote most of his novels, in the 1830s and 1840s, gave him historical perspective.

Most of his novels are set in the 1820s, under the Restoration, while written following the Revolution of 1830 that put an end to the Restoration, so that he looks back at an era completed, and can analyze all the more sharply its meaning. He takes in this manner Walter Scott's practice of the historical novel, designed to give a picture of life in England in the twelfth century or in Scotland in the eighteenth century, and updates it to an almost contemporary period that can nonetheless be grasped as past, as an epoch completed.

A Question of France

I could pick almost any Balzac novel to illustrate his uses of history: it permeates everywhere. But rather than the better-known *Père Goriot* or *Lost Illusions*, let me evoke another story that I recently rediscovered, which in rereading seems to me eloquently on point: *The Collection of Antiquities (Le Cabinet des antiques)*. In this short and effective novel, Balzac again explores the dynamic links of the provinces to Paris, but now with greater emphasis on what goes on in provincial life. The story unfolds in a Norman town that isn't named, though it's assumed, from the predecessor novel *The Old Maid (La Vieille fille)*, to be Alençon. The "antiquities" are the group of unrepentant Legitimist nobles who gather regularly at the townhouse of the Marquis d'Esgrignon, a man in his seventies who did not emigrate with the Bourbons but rather remained to tend to the family estates, only to see them fall into ruin. He bears among his many forenames that of "Carol," which evokes a Frankish ancestor of the very deep past who defeated the Gauls. His family traces its lineage without interruption from those ancient times. He owns a château outside Alençon that has become uninhabitable from disuse and decay. He has barely enough money to support himself and his unmarried half-sister, Mademoiselle Armande, and the pride of the family, the young Comte Victurnien d'Esgrignon. Past history is ingrained in the Marquis: his house, his friends, his rituals, his speech and beliefs all represent a world that exists no longer except in the ideology of these leftovers from the Ancien Régime. As in William Faulkner's novels of the southern United States, the past is not past for these nobles. They act as if the maintenance of caste boundaries and class privileges were the sum of existence. Yet they don't have the income, which traditionally would have come from their landed property, to support their pretentions. They lean heavily on the notary Maître Chesnel, whom they treat as a kind of old family servant, and who is supposed to find in the debris of their estates the wherewithal to keep their lives going.

Chesnel in his eagerness to restore the family fortunes has proposed that Mlle Armande marry the local bourgeois notable du Croisier. This mésalliance is rejected with indignation by the Marquis and by Armande herself. She devotes herself to taking the place of Victurnien's dead mother, and raising him with full awareness of what it means to bear the Esgrignon name. But her rejection sparks the unrelenting enmity of du Croisier toward the d'Esgrignon family and all of the "antiquities." Du Croisier becomes the leader of the "liberal" party in Alençon—the opposition: we are now under the Restoration. And he cultivates Victurnien, assuring him that his purse is at the young man's disposal. Victurnien in fact, raised to think he has the freedom from restraint of an Ancien Régime *libertin,* accumulates gambling debts and, more than that, requires hush money for several young woman he has seduced. Victurnien must be sent to Paris, to the Court, where, the old Marquis is certain, the king will give him a position simply because of the name he bears: Admiral in the Navy, General in the Army, or an ambassadorship. Even Victurnien is aware that the world doesn't work that way anymore: you need to be admitted to one of the schools that train you for those positions. The Restoration hasn't wholly liquidated the Napoleonic creed of "career open to talent," enshrined in the educational system that Napoleon largely created.

But Victurnien happily goes to Paris, with all the money Chesnel can scrape up, where his name does open his way to acquaintance with the young roués of the time: de Marsay, Rastignac, de Trailles and others. And then he meets the ravishing Diane de Maufrigneuse (later Princesse de Cadignan, heroine of the novella about her "secrets") and becomes her lover. She lives separated from her husband and she too has debts. Debt accumulates. Du Croisier sees his opportunity to complete the ruin of the family. He writes Victurnien a letter denying him any further loans, but he intentionally leaves a large blank space between the body of the letter and his signature. Victurnien falls into the trap: he cuts off the lower part of the letter and inserts, above the signature, the language of a *lettre de change*—a kind of i.o.u. that circulated like a bank check—to his own order from du Croisier. He collects the money from the Keller bank. But now he is guilty of criminal fraud and will be arrested. In the drama of his arrest and trial come to bear the struggle between the old nobility and the rising bourgeoisie, as well as the possibility of corrupting the workings of justice—and the possible long-term solution to the conflicts.

When Chesnel goes to plead with du Croisier to hush up the affair and find a way to free Victurinen, now in prison, he pleads the honor of an old family and that of his homeland. Du Croisier replies that this is not the point. What is the point, asks Chesnel, astonished. And du Croisier has a speech that carries great weight:

> Monsieur Chesnel, it's a question of France! it's a question of the nation, of the people, it's a matter of teaching your noble gentlemen that there is such a thing as justice, laws, a bourgeoisie and a minor nobility that are worth just as much as you! You don't ravage ten wheat fields to hunt a hare, you don't bring dishonor into families by seducing poor girls, you should not despise people who are just as good as you, you don't make fun of them over ten years' time, without these deeds swelling to produce an avalanche, and these avalanches falling to crush and bury the nobility. You want to return to the old order of things, you want to tear up the social contract, and the constitution in which our rights are written...[7]

Balzac here puts in the mouth of a reasonably unattractive character an act of accusation that is entirely justified, in the context of the novel as in life outside the novel in the world of the Restoration. The refusal of the Restoration to accept changes that were happening, indeed had already happened, its attempt to turn the clock back to Ancien Régime standard time, created an impasse that could only lead to another revolution, that of 1830—which ought logically to have led to a republic but instead produced a hybrid bourgeois constitutional monarchy that would come to grief in 1848. However admirable the d'Esgrignons and their sense of history, they are relics, and their fate is only given a temporary respite.

At the climax of Victurnien's troubles, where it appears he may be on the verge of a long sentence to prison, Diane de Maufrigneuse arrives, dressed in a man's clothing (which only makes her the more adorable and seductive), bringing the sum of one hundred thousand francs from the king "to buy the innocence of Victurnien, if his adversary can be corrupted. If we fail, I also have

poison, to take him away from everything, even indictment."
(P 4:1077/G 306) Admirable alternatives! The king doesn't want
the old nobility besmirched and sent to prison. But Diane—who
knows that her liaison with Victurnien is at an end—mocks and
explodes the beliefs of these antique provincial nobles. She tells
Victurnien that his only long-term solution lies in marriage to a
rich bourgeoise. Mlle Armande reacts against such a mésalliance,
and Diane laughs in her face:

> "Are you all insane here?" said the duchesse. You want then to
> remain in the fifteenth century when we are in the nineteenth?
> My dear children, there is no more nobility, there is merely an
> aristocracy. Napoleon's Civil Code killed off our titles of nobility
> the way cannon killed off feudalism. You will be much more noble
> than you are now when you have money. Marry whomever you
> want, Victurnien, you will ennoble your wife, that's the most solid
> of the privileges that still belong the French nobility.
>
> (P 4:1092/G 306–7)

These words from one of the truly great ladies of the Faubourg
Saint-German merit attention.

What Diane, like her creator, understands is that in nineteenth-
century France you can continue to behave like an aristocracy, to
claim social privilege and prestige, but you no longer belong to a
closed system of nobility. New blood and, especially, new money
is required to keep the upper class going. If one were to examine
the root cause, you would no doubt find it in the abolition of primogeniture, the *droit d'aînesse,* by the Revolution, which then was
inscribed in the Civil Code: a father's legacy was to be equally
shared among his sons. Napoleon modified the legislation somewhat by introducing the *majorat,* a system for acquiring property
attached to a title that was inheritable. Under Charles X—far more

reactionary than his older brother Louis XVIII, to whom he succeeded in 1824—there was a partial attempt to reestablish primogeniture but it didn't get far. As he and the *ultras*—the true reactionaries—argued, you cannot perpetuate a wealthy and powerful nobility unless families can keep their estates together, passed on to the eldest son, while the younger sons were expected to join the military or enter religious orders. Balzac, who several times was tempted to run for election to the Assembly himself, entered the debate in 1824 with a brochure arguing in favor of the *droit d'aînesse* as the only way to maintain the great fortunes and the great families of France.[8] They, he understands, represent the other side of the page from the ambitious young adventurers that will come to fill the pages of his novels in the following decade. But history was not headed toward the revival of primogeniture.

So Diane de Maufrigneuse is clairvoyant and logical in her argument that someone like Victurnien d'Esgrignon can thrive only by joining his noble name to a bourgeois fortune. "Victurnien, marry Mlle. Duval, marry whomever you wish, she will be Marquise d'Esgrignon every bit as much as I am Duchesse de Maufrigneuse." (P 4:1093/G 307–8) Chesnel dies and then the old Marquis—whose last words are: "The Gauls have won!" referring to the historian Augustin Thierry's claim that the French nobility descends from the Franks and the plebeians from the Gauls. Victurnien fights a duel with du Croisier, who cannot abide that the young man has escaped prison, and is seriously wounded. He recovers, but left alone, impoverished, and bored, following the Revolution of 1830 Victurnien does marry Mlle Duval, the niece of his enemy du Croisier, who brings him a dowry of three million francs. It's a realization of Diane's advice. It's also a triumph for du Croisier, who has bought his way into a noble family, and established his position as the only power in Alençon. And it points the way forward to a fusion of aristocracy and bourgeoisie that Balzac found necessary even while he lamented the decline of the great families.

The Smell of Money

The movement from an economy and a polis rooted in land owning, essentially agricultural wealth in a quasi-feudal system, to one founded on the circulation of money is one of the large subjects and structural principles of *The Human Comedy*. Over and over again we learn about the status of fortunes, their acquisition, or their absence, or the dilapidation of family wealth over time. At the start of the novella *Sarrasine*, for instance, the narrator overhears guests at the splendid party put on by the Lanty speculating on the origins of the family fortune. He cites the aphorism attributed to Vespasian: money has no smell. In Paris, he says, "even coins spotted with blood or with filth betray nothing and represent everything. So long as high society can put a figure on your fortune, you are classified among those of equal wealth, and no one asks to see your letters of nobility, because everyone knows how little those are worth. In a town in which social problems are resolved by algebraic equations, fortune hunters have chance on their side. Even supposing this family had bohemian origins, it was so rich and attractive that high society could well pardon its little mysteries."[9] In the case of *Sarrasine*, to be sure, we discover that the family fortune has a strange and not entirely reputable origin: in the fortune accumulated by Zambinella, the castrato singer who was Mme de Lanty's uncle. But if the narrator and his friend

Mme de Rochefide to whom he confides the story care about this origin, society doesn't. Money, especially when there is lots of it, doesn't smell.

Which doesn't stop Balzac and his characters from trying to sniff at it, to discover its origins, to situate it in the social scene. One of Balzac's first serious expositors, Hippolyte Taine, claimed that the true hero of *The Human Comedy* was the twenty-franc piece, and money in fact is omnipresent throughout Balzac's world. For his young heroes, newly arrived from the provinces and intent upon making it in Paris, the calculation of what everything costs and how much they will need is paramount. When Lucien de Rubempré takes a first stroll in the Tuileries Garden, to discover the world of "necessary superfluities," the crucial importance of accessories such as cufflinks, cravats, gilt buttons on one's waistcoat, riding crops, lorgnons, and on up to horses, carriages, and grooms, he understands they cost a fortune to acquire. When he is snubbed by high society, his reaction is: "Money, at any price!" When Eugène de Rastignac discovers the objects of his desires at the first ball he attends, at the Vicomtesse de Beauséant's, his mentor Vautrin calculates exactly what he will need: "A million, and straightaway!" Vautrin goes on to explain—in figures that have been validated in our time by economist Thomas Piketty—that his salary as a lawyer, even if he makes his way upwards through means honest and not quite honest, will never be equal to his desires. Earned income won't do it; he needs an inheritance, and that's most easily got by marrying a wealthy woman, or at least one with expectations of a big legacy.

Vautrin's plan for Rastignac includes homicide—recall he will have young Jean-Frédéric Taillefer killed in a duel by a master swordsman so that his sister Victorine will become her father's sole heir, and she is already sweet on Rastignac. Rastignac rejects this plan as too overtly criminal. But the way he makes his fortune, as we've seen already, involves forms of corruption only less obviously murderous. He becomes the straw man in the speculations of his mistress's husband, which net him a small fortune, and then marries the daughter of the household. Rastignac's fortune and ultimately his great worldly success derive from his choice of the banker's wife as his mistress, and the banker's decision that he is useful to financial schemes.

Nucingen again steps forward as the most characteristic figure of the new age. In his hands everything becomes money. You might say his goal is total liquidity, amassing capital that is not in landed property but financial instruments that are completely fungible, money that can be moved around quickly, made to disappear and reappear in new guises. The making of his money always appears to be slightly obscured—because it is far from straightforward. It seems to depend to a large degree on fake bankruptcies that allow him to sell off overpriced assets and repurchase them at fire sale prices. His final coup of this sort comes in July 1830, when King Charles X on July 25 issues his "three decrees," the *trois ordonnances,* which restrict freedom of the press, dissolve the recently elected National Assembly, institute new electoral laws favorable to the aristocracy, and call for a new election in September. Realizing at once that Charles has doomed his rule, Nucingen sells short and then cleans up after the Revolution takes place at the end of July. The July Revolution will make of him a Peer of the Realm and Grand Officer of the Légion d'Honneur.

Nucingen is a perfect illustration of Karl Marx's famous characterization of capitalism in *The Communist Manifesto*:

Constant revolutionising of production, uninterrupted distur-
bance of all social conditions, everlasting uncertainty and agitation
distinguish the bourgeois epoch from all earlier ones. All fixed,
fast-frozen relations, with their train of ancient and venerable prejudices and opinions, are swept away, all new-formed ones become
antiquated before they can ossify. All that is solid melts into air, all
that is holy is profaned, and man is at last compelled to face with
sober senses his real conditions of life, and his relations with his
kind.[10]

That actually could stand as a good summary of *The Human Comedy*
as a whole. Yet the melting of all that is solid into money produces
reaction as well, for instance in the case of Lucien. By the time he
has been rescued from his intended suicide by Vautrin, disguised
as the Spanish priest Carlos Herrera, and returned to Paris social life,
he needs to find a permanent footing for his precarious existence
as Vautrin's creature: someone about whom figures in society ask,
what's the source of his money? Vautrin works out a plot for Lucien:
he needs to buy back the alienated estate of his mother, an aristocrat
named de Rubempré reduced to indigence by the Revolution and
then wife of the bourgeois pharmacist Chardon. Then Lucien will
be able to marry Clotilde de Grandlieu, daughter of one of the great
houses of the Faubourg Saint-German, whose figure looks like an
asparagus but who would bring him a fortune in dowry. But Lucien
needs a cool million to buy back the Rubempré estate. Where to
get the funds? Vautrin has it all worked out: he will sell Lucien's
beautiful mistress Esther—former prostitute, redeemed by her love
for Lucien—to Nucingen who glimpsed her by moonlight in the
Bois de Vincennes and at once fell head over heels in love with her.
Vautrin's first move is to sequester Esther so she cannot be found
by Nucingen's agents, then to sell her off gradually, promising

rendezvous that don't happen, alleging debts that Nucingen has to pay before he can have her, finally arranging a stipend of thirty thousand francs for her from stocks, which Esther promptly sells in order to realize the capital that Lucien needs—before killing herself, as she has promised she would do, after one night in Nucingen's arms.

It's all totally sordid, and will come apart in the most dire manner when Vautrin and Lucien are arrested for Esther's death, and the cash she left under her pillow for Lucien is stolen by servants. Lucien will hang himself with his cravat from the bars of his prison cell, and Vautrin, now returned to his baptismal name, Jacques Collin, will surrender to the judge who has been interrogating him—and pass to the other side, to become a police detective who will devote himself to a future as that "agent of order and repression." And as Vautrin/Collin will explain to the judge at the very end, his criminal career has merely been a sort of mirror of Nucingen's. The banker has done "legally," with the acceptance of society, what Collin has done in the shadows of the underworld. In his description, Nucingen is

> a man covered in secret infamies, a monster who has committed in the world of finance such crimes that every gold piece of his fortune is soaked in the tears of some family, a Nucingen who has been a Jacques Collin legally and in the world of money. Really you know as well as I his bankruptcies and the actions for which he could be hung.[11]

The interchangeability of criminal and cop that allows Collin to finish his career as chief of the Sûreté (something like the FBI) appears to be matched by the lack of distinction between banker and criminal. Capitalism is founded in fraud, and all its products are likely to be contaminated.

In addition to the banker Nucingen, who figures in so many novels of *The Human Comedy,* there is the usurer Gobseck, equally omnipresent. He represents older forms of accumulation and circulation of wealth, someone who lends out money (at exorbitant interest) rather than a speculator in industrial undertakings, such as mines, canals, railroads. But Gobseck, sometimes described as a "capitalist," is presented as something of a philosopher of money. "Gold," he says, "represents all human forces."[12] It is a kind of demonic force in society. "Isn't life a kind of machine to which money provides movement?...Gold is the spiritualism of contemporary societies." Gobseck describes himself as a "poet" who sits unmoving in his room while all the dramas of Paris, moved by the need for money, come to enact themselves before his eyes. Unlike Nucingen, presented as the type of the Alsatian banker, Gobseck achieves a kind of special status as a hidden demiurge who makes things happen in the world while he is unmoved.

I noted earlier Oscar Wilde's aphorism: "The nineteenth century, as we know it, is largely an invention of Balzac."[13] If I have dwelt so much on money—but how not to in Balzac's world?—it's because his understanding of the coming of the cash nexus is new among novelists and unrivaled in its perception of how the whole of society has been permeated by the struggle to get ahead. It is of course a kind of conservative nostalgia to believe that in Ancien Régime society everyone was happily pigeonholed in his social place, a harmonious organic whole. That régime did, after all, end in revolution, and Balzac fully understands why even if his stated ideology deplores it. He knows he is himself a product of the new régime, with its ostensible freedom to make the most of your talents. What he most of all laments, I think, is the loss of a principle of paternal authority. The regicide of 1793 deprived France of her symbolic father, and that plays out in many different ways throughout *The Human Comedy*, perhaps most clearly in the case of Lucien de Rubempré. As Vautrin will put it to Rastignac, cynically and perceptively, "There are no principles, there are only events; there are no laws, only circumstances." (P 3:144/S 116) Rastignac will learn his version of that, as Bixiou maintains in *The House of Nucingen*: there isn't such a thing as virtue, only circumstances in which you may be able to act virtuously. But Vautrin's lesson reaches beyond his immediate pupil: it offers an overarching and frightening vision of modernity. Dostoevsky admired, translated, and learned from Balzac. When we confront the portrait of modernity given in the two novelists, we realize that Vautrin's disabused statement provides us with an earlier and more secular version of Ivan Karamazov's claim: in the absence of God, all is permitted.

Amplest Sweeps

But Balzac's dynamic picture of money and the struggles for dominance in emerging capitalist society doesn't constitute the whole of his claim to give us the shape of time, for his time. I borrow that phrase from Marcel Proust: at the end of *In Search of Lost Time*, Marcel discovers that his vocation must be to write a book that will have "the shape of time."[14] Proust always is generous in his praise of Balzac, whose example underlies the ambitions of the *Search* as portrait of a society. Another modernist master yet more thorough and explicit in acknowledgement of his debt to Balzac is Henry James, who claims that Balzac is a master of representing "the lapse of time, the duration of the subject."[15]

He goes on to say: "No one begins, to my sense, to handle the time-element and produce the time-effect with the authority of Balzac in his amplest sweeps." As so often, James is on the mark as an analyst of narrative. "Amplest sweeps" captures well the way Balzac gives dramatic summaries of a situation, of a moment in history and how it came to be that way. *A Murky Business* and *The Member from Arcis* and *The Cabinet of Antiquities* depend on such moments. In fact, all of Balzac's novels do: it's his premise that you have to know the socio-historical coordinates of the plots and of the persons, why they are present at certain places at given times. As Lukács noted, what look like coincidences are in fact deeply motivated by the historical forces at play. Moments of drama that may at first seem contrived really, as you read on, seem inevitable: Lucien the poet come to Paris was bound to meet a journalist, who would offer him the path of corruption. Rastignac seems fated to have found a Delphine de Nucingen, who can satisfy the need for love and the need for money: speaking love to Delphine is productive of cash. Eugénie Grandet's position as the sheltered daughter of a miser in the provincial town of Saumur is a magnet for the exploitative young man. Victurnien d'Esgrignon's upbringing as spoiled scion of the *Antiques* in Alençon and need of support for his prodigal life propels him toward the trap du Croisier has laid for him. Ursule Mirouët's unprotected condition will allow her legacy to be taken from her. And so on. These are all breathtaking stories that offer significant understandings of the historical moment.

And then there is *The Human Comedy* itself as a conception. It wasn't there from the outset. It was only gradually, as he published individual novels in the 1830s, that he discovered the possibility of linking one to another, with characters returning from novel to novel, to create a sense of a fully furnished society. It is only in 1842 that Balzac writes a preface, his *Avant-Propos* or "General Introduction" to *The Human Comedy*, laying out its ambitions and principles of organization. That document is in some ways a pot-boiler, an effort to create sales for a reprint of previously published novels, as well as a promissory note for those to come: a vast work comprising 101 titles, which he would not quite complete before his death. I don't believe the *Avant-Propos* needs to be taken so seriously as many critics have. But if it isn't a definitive guide to *The Human Comedy*, it does do justice to the ambitions of the project, especially the tripartite division of the work into "Studies of Manners," "Philosophical Studies," and "Analytical Studies." The philosophical studies were to explain the causes of the social effects we encounter in the studies of manners—*moeurs,* which in French encompasses more than we usually mean by manners: ways of being, we might say. And then the analytical studies were to show the large principles that underly both effects and causes, the *ultima ratio mundi.* Since the analytic studies remain fragmentary we can't say that the structural design of *The Human Comedy* is fulfilled. I'm not sure we would be happier if it were: while some of the analytic studies are wonderfully evocative in their attempts to provide a kind of semiotics of modern life, they are not necessarily wholly persuasive. The text that seems the keystone of the analytical studies, the *Theory of Movement (Théorie de la démarche)* attempts an analysis of the expressivity of all human movement. It appears at once interestingly suggestive and quite mad. It's not without significance that Balzac's obsessed thinkers, inventors, innovators in art and science all go over the brink. The chemist/

alchemist Balthasar Claës of *the Search for the Absolute* (*La recherche de l'Absolu*) destroys fortune and family in his quest for the ultimate particle of matter. The painter Frenhofer pushes his research into expressive representation to the point where he makes his masterpiece canvas illegible. The philosopher Louis Lambert becomes catatonic on the eve of his marriage, attempts self-castration, and ends up aphasic, unable to express the putatively profound thoughts that are passing through his head.

Let me close by evoking what I hope will not seem too preposterous a comparison that at times occurs to me in reading Balzac. Shakespeare's history plays, and especially the four that have come to be known as the "Henriad"—*Richard II, Henry IV Part One* and *Part Two, Henry V*—in their different genre and very different tonality provide something of the same historical sweep that Balzac aims at in his more disorganized and prolix manner. The Henriad takes us from a world that still is founded in feudal hierarchy and custom, dramatized at the outset of *Richard II* in the duel between Mowbray and Bolingbroke that King Richard will, ominously for his rule, interrupt, sending the two combatants into exile, violating custom in an assertion of his absolute and arbitrary rule. The two parts of *Henry IV* show the results of Richard's overthrow by Bolingbroke, now become King: England is torn apart by internal strife, legitimacy is in question, the king is suffering, and the heir apparent, Prince Hal, seemingly gone to riot in the stews of London under the tutelage of Falstaff. Then when Prince Hal ascends the throne in *Henry V* and leads the English to victory at Agincourt, we have a new kind of ruler, one who has established his legitimacy not by inheritance and tradition but by military victory and the appeal of vigorous leadership. We are in a new world.

A new world is where Balzac the novelist situates himself, and he plots out how it came to be, by no means in celebration of its advent though with a sense of what necessitates it. That's a large part of what I found so exhilarating as I read more and more in *The Human Comedy*, and a key to why I keep coming back to Balzac. He sees the France of his time as the product of its recent history. He not only understands that history, he builds it into his fiction. He can't bring a new character on stage without telling us how he or she fits into that history, what their antecedents were, what they have been doing in historical time before coming on stage. You don't have to be an historian of early nineteenth-century France to understand them: Balzac will fill in the needed facts for you. But you need to be aware that these characters are situated in history, that each of them bears the shape of time. The dimension of temporality is always there, determining persons and their actions, determining also the way we read, the kind of joy of mastery that comes with understanding the meaning of time.

5

TO SAY EVERYTHING

Rousseau's *Confessions* have long seemed to me the key moment of entry into modernity, into the world we still inhabit, with its ostensible emphasis on sincerity, authenticity, the individual's identity and the need to speak fully of its inner desires as well as its misdeeds. Rousseau was crucial in my attempt to understand the role of the voluntary and the involuntary confession in law as in literature.[1] He stands as well behind Balzac's understanding of modernity, its ethics, and aesthetics. At a couple of key moments of the *Confessions* Rousseau pauses to apologize for the lengthy details he has put the reader through, and to justify his need for going on at such length about trivial incidents. In the most famous of these moments, Rousseau claims that he wants to make his "soul transparent to the reader's eye." In order to do so, he must show himself from all points of view, shed light on every day's happenings, "so that nothing that occurs escapes his attention, so he can judge by himself of the principle that produces it."[2] Like Rousseau's preface to his novel, *The New Héloise*, this appears a justification of a detailed realism that is designed to turn the reader into interpreter and judge. The other moment comes early on, in Book Two; it needs quoting at greater length:

In the project I have undertaken to show myself in my entirety to the public it matters that nothing of me remain obscure or hidden; I have to hold myself incessantly before his eyes; to have him follow me in all the wayward movements of my heart, in all the hidden corners of my life; so that he not lose sight of me for a single moment, so that, finding in my narrative the slightest gap, the smallest empty space, and asking himself: What did he do during that time? he not accuse me of not wanting to say everything.[3]

The ideal of "saying everything": *tout dire*. Its most obvious exponent—clearly a disciple of Rousseau—is the Marquis de Sade, who in his manic books written (and when destroyed, rewritten) feels driven to detail all the possible crimes that he can think of, none of them impermissible because "nature" has given us the means to carry them out, and nature is the great non-principle to which he adheres, in a twisted imitation of Rousseau. The *One Hundred Twenty Days of Sodom* desperately tries to register all possible combinations of crime, torture, pain. At the end, it is reduced to simple listings of what it doesn't have time to detail. Saying all is not so easy.

Describing the Known World

Balzac is not writing confessional autobiography (though there are recognizable autobiographical moments in his novels, especially when he recounts the unhappy childhood of unloved young men, abandoned by their mothers) but in his project of giving a total representation of the society of his time—French society would be the author, he merely the secretary he claims in the *Avant-Propos*—he is driven to something like the Rousseauian or Sadean project: the need to say everything. This everything isn't just a matter of coverage, making sure you have registered all the different social categories, though there is certainly much of that in Balzac's expanding list of "scenes": of provincial life, of Parisian life, of private life, of country life, of military life, and his shifting of his texts from one category to another. But what interests me more is his need, once launched upon a subject, a person, a house, a fortune, to say everything about it that he can. That's obvious to any reader in his descriptive presentations of persons, places, and things. Many Balzac novels begin with the kind of exhaustive description that we today find almost illegible, though in Balzac's case descriptions are often redeemed by their sheer manic intensity. For example (it's an obvious one) the description of the Pension Vauquer at the outset of *Père Goriot*, which tells us of the greasy dining room and its matching person, Madame Vauquer, and of all the lodgers in the various rooms, from the most comfortable to the barest garret. The furniture of the dining room alone deserves penetrating attention:

Indestructible pieces of furniture, banned elsewhere, have landed there like debris of civilization in the hospice for Incurables. Here you would see a barometer, with a monk who emerges when it rains, horrible engravings that take away your appetite, in varnished frames with gilt edging; a tortoise-shell clock incrusted with copper; a green tiled stove, Argand lamps smeared with oil and dust, a long table covered with an oilcloth so greasy that a playful diner can write his name on it using his finger as a pen, wounded chairs, piteous little straw place mats that are always unwinding without ever completely disappearing, then miserable footwarmers, caved in, with broken doors, their wood charred. To detail to you how much this furniture is old, cracked, rotten, trembling, one-armed, one-eyed, invalid, moribund, would need a description that would delay too much this story, and that people in a hurry would never forgive. The red tile floor is full of valleys produced by rubbing and repainting. In sum, here reigns misery without poetry; a misery of poverty, concentrated, threadbare. If it is not yet covered in mud, it's bespattered; if it isn't yet in rags and tatters, it is going to fall into rot.   (P 3:53–4/S 10)

This inventory of things might be unbearable were it not that the observer's imagination takes off, heats up, lets itself be carried forward by the implications of its own words and images. Furniture is fit only for the hospice of Incurables. It is cracked, rotten, trembling, one-armed—so far one can easily envision chairs in such a state—and then "one-eyed." The one-eyed (*borgne*) seems to be called forth by the preceding one-armed (*manchot*). One-armed, though most often used describe people who have lost an arm, can easily be applied to a damaged arm chair. But one-eyed? We have moved into a kind of evocative animation of the furniture, that continues with "invalid" and "moribund" (*expirant*). We have moved from the visual inspection of dining-room furniture to an evocation of someone on his deathbed. The descriptive prose has come alive through its metaphoric evocations and transformations. Then comes Balzac's nod to the reader: enough description, on with the story. Though he can't quite stop without calling attention to the worn floor, and summing up with a flourish on the kind of misery found in the Pension.

The world described is the world come alive, at least when Balzac is writing at full heat, attentive not only to things but to their metaphysical implications. There are too many examples to choose from. Here for instance is the bedroom of the actress Coralie who in *Lost Illusions* has fallen in love with Lucien and installed him in the apartment furnished for her by her official lover and keeper the silk merchant Camusot, whom she will soon dismiss though she can ill afford to do so. Her maid Bérénice lights the candles, and Lucien sees for the first time the room in which he spent the night in Coralie's arms:

> By the light of the candles, Lucien, bewildered, thought himself transported into a fairytale palace. The richest fabrics from the Cocon d'Or had been chosen by Camusot for the wall hangings and window curtains. The poet trod on a royal carpet. The muted light glanced off carvings of rosewood furniture that reflected its gleams. The white marble chimneypiece shone with the most costly baga-telles. The bedside rug was in swansdown bordered with sable. Slippers of black velvet lined in purple silk spoke of the pleasures that awaited the poet of the *Marguerites*. A delicious lamp hung from the ceiling draped in silk. Everywhere flower stands displayed choice flowers, beautiful white heather, unscented camellias. Everywhere lay images of innocence. How to imagine an actress and the ways of the theatre here?   (P 5:413/ML 330)

Coralie's room, got up at Camusot's expense, is a conscious repre-sentation of love, sex, the voluptuous, a kind of simulation of a seductive innocence that Lucien, it seems, senses to be out of synch with the true life of the actress. Yet it is more accurately another piece of theatre, a stage set for acts of love that profit from the simulated innocence of Coralie. Bérénice immediately calls attention to the artifice when, noticing Lucien's astonishment at the room, she tells him in a wheedling voice: "It's nice, isn't it?...Aren't you better off making love here than in an attic? Don't let her do anything rash." Bérénice understands the need for the artifice, and the need for Camusot's cash to make it real. She fears Coralie's passion for Lucien will make her throw caution to the winds and break with Camusot—which in fact she will. That eventually produces a scene where Lucien and Coralie sit in a room that has been stripped of its furnishings by the bailiffs on behalf of their creditors: "there wasn't any object in gold or silver left, or anything of real value" (P 5:495/ML 424). Coralie falls in love, for the first time in her life, deeply, fully with Lucien. And that is her undoing, the end to the representation she as an actress needs. It's like the "paradox" of Lucien's newspaper articles: if you believe in what you say, you can't do it effectively. If you give up "love" for love, you are reduced to penury. Eventually Coralie will exceed her forces trying to make money on the stage to pay off the debts that she and Lucien accumulate. She dies, and her headstone in Père-Lachaise cemetery tells us that she was only nineteen years old.

Place as representation finds its confirmation by way of a negative version when Lucien visits the room where the journalist Etienne Lousteau lives. He reflects that the misery of the young trying to make it in Paris pursues him everywhere. But whereas in Daniel d'Arthez's cold and threadbare apartment it was a "decent misery":

> Here that misery was sinister. A walnut bedstead without curtains at the foot of which grimaced a shabby second-hand rug; in the window, curtains yellowed from cigar smoke and that of a chimney that didn't draw; on the mantelpiece a Carcel lamp, a present from Florine [another actress, Lousteau's mistress] as yet escaped going to the pawnshop; a faded mahogany chest of drawers, a table covered with papers, two or three discarded quill pens on it, no other books than those brought in that day: such was the furniture of this room stripped of any objects of value, which instead offered an ignoble assemblage of broken-down boots gaping a corner, old socks worn to ribbons; and in another corner, cigar stubs, dirty handkerchiefs, shirts that had seen two editions, cravats that had known three. It was in fact a journalist's bivouac, furnished with negative things and of the strangest nudity that one can imagine.   (P 5:350/ML 256)

The description rolls on, mentioning dueling swords and pistols—the acrimony of journalism often led to duels, and Lucien will fight one with Michel Chrestien over Lucien's review of d'Arthez's novel—and razors and three side chairs and two armchairs "scarcely worthy of the shabbiest furnished apartment houses in the street." The narrator sums up:

> This room, at once dirty and sad, told of a life without repose and without dignity: you slept there, you worked there under time pressure, it was inhabited by force, you felt the need to leave it. What a difference between this cynical disorder and the clean, decent poverty of d'Arthez!...But this warning in the guise of a memory went unheeded, for Etienne made a joke to mask the nudity of Vice.
>
> "Here's my kennel, my big show is in the rue de Bondy, in the new apartment that our druggist has furnished for Florine that we're inaugurating this evening."

I have thought long and often about this passage, which gives the essence of a certain descriptive art. Lousteau's literary bivouac is furnished with "negative things," things that have a minus value: they have no standing in the marketplace, no exchange value; no one wants them, they represent nothing, in contrast to Coralie's love nest. Anything of potential value, such as the Carcel lamp gifted to Lousteau by Florine, is on its way to the pawnshop. The heaps of clothes are like used up books, and in fact the only books visible have arrived that day—since Lousteau at once sells all the review copies he comes by to the second-hand booksellers along the Seine. How the narrator/observer knows that these books have arrived only today isn't specified—it's part of the dynamic, demonic life of Balzacian objects, always in movement between purchase, sale, putting in hock. There is a fair amount of moralizing here: the journalist's life is without dignity and repose. But what deprives it of dignity are largely the values of the marketplace. Consider: "negative things" and "the nudity of vice." It's vice because there is nothing of market value in the room. Vice is the failure of accumulation, the failure to furnish your life with luxury items, with excess valuations.

Lousteau seems instinctively to understand Lucien's reaction (the narrator's also?) to his miserable fifth-floor walkup: he makes a joke to mask the nudity of vice. And that joke is about his show—the French word is *représentation*—in the rue de Bondy, where Florine's official lover and keeper Matifat has furnished her a splendid apartment. "Representation," here as with Coralie, has to be paid for by rich businessmen. Lousteau and Lucien may be the chosen objects of their women's true love, but they are themselves only actors on the stage set provided by those who have money. Does the nudity of vice suggest that the "representations" furnished by rich bourgeois who keep actress mistresses are to be thought virtue? Not quite, but the mirror opposite is true: nudity equals vice in Balzac's world, whatever lip service may be paid to "decent poverty." If you don't have furnishings of market value surrounding you, you are vulnerable to the accusation of the vice of nudity, of having no representation to give of yourself. Balzac, ever in debt, spent with famous extravagance on the furnishings of the places in which he lived, as well as on such personal accessories as his famous cane with its jewel-incrusted head. That inventory of the house on the rue Fortunée I mentioned earlier reads as an effort to keep all the wolves of the world at bay by surrounding himself and his bride-to-be with the most expensive furniture and stuffs that money could buy. There is decidedly a fear, in Balzac, of falling through one's representations—the accumulation of things that insulate you against the threatening world outside—to that nudity of vice. And that's of course what Lucien is reduced to at the end of his spectacular rise and sudden fall in

Paris journalism. He doesn't have a sou for his return, on foot, to the benighted provincial city where he began: Coralie's maid Bérénice goes out to prostitute herself to raise the money he needs. That's the "final stigma" of his Paris experience. Before, of course, he returns in the sequel novel as the protégé of Jacques Collin, alias Vautrin, now reincarnated as the Spanish priest Carlos Herrera.

Balzac's long, narrativized, often manic descriptions offer one version of trying to "say everything" about the physical world as it has been created by and represents people. The ambition of the *Avant-Propos* to write the story of contemporary France through its "men, women, and things" gives pride of place to things. Things are not simply there; they are acquired by men and women to represent themselves. And representation always rests on money. Without it, representation collapses to the kind of sub-zero status we see in Lousteau's room, where description is reduced to enumerating "negative things," to come out with a result of nudity. You could say, I imagine, that the nineteenth century on the whole sought to fill all the voids: if Directoire and Empire styles remain somewhat spare and restrained, after that it's a piling on of furnishings, draperies, accessories, until you reach the Second Empire's massive overstuffing of rooms. There comes to be a kind of fear of the void, which you feel first in Balzac. To be without things of value is to be exposed, to be naked.

To say everything means wholly furnishing a world: the houses and furnishings that human beings acquire to live in an otherwise unaccommodating world, how they clothe and decorate themselves, are to the penetrating observer legible clues to who they are. The human beings themselves of course multiply across *The Human Comedy* in the effort to account for all enterprises, occupations, professions, ways of acting in the world. Balzac's ambition to be the secretary of society meant he needed to think in terms of representative types—the lawyer, the doctor, the country priest, the prostitute—but this didn't really suit his ways of understanding very well. He feels most at ease in the individual case, putting pressure on the single figure to make it release its full potential. He may offer Maître Derville as the type of the lawyer; he appears in many novels, always as a figure of competence and probity. There are other lawyers, Delbcq is an example, who are largely unscrupulous. But they aren't presented as representatives of their class so much as they are individuals who help us to understand the class. Antoinette de Langeais, in *The Duchesse de Langeais*, is said to represent the Faubourg Saint-Germain nobility during the Restoration, a narcissistic, selfish coquette with high regard for self and caste but little understanding of true emotion. But her ultimately tragic love plot is about the awakening of something different, something that cannot be accounted for by her social representativity alone. And this is true I think of all the fictional people that matter in *The Human Comedy*.

Gatherings

Balzac's impossible desire to people his world fully, to say every imaginable person, can maybe be best grasped in those moments where a number of them gather together. There are many such moments. As his great work took on momentum, there could be more: he could call upon previously created beings to gather in a salon or at the Opéra or in a boardinghouse. The Pension Vauquer of *Père Goriot* is an early instance of the "grand hotel" technique that would be used many times over in later novels and films: the different rooms of a building housing different characters who will have to interact from their simple proximity, though boardinghouse interaction is inevitably more intimate than, say, the apartment building of Emile Zola's *Pot-Bouille*, where it's mainly the servants who know everything that's going on in the building. There are social gatherings, such as Félicité des Touches' late-night supper in *Another Study of Womankind*, which I have already discussed. Here it is the cream of Parisian society, not in terms of social hierarchy—such a bourgeois as Dr. Horace Bianchon is a principal figure—but of accomplishment and intelligence. Then there is the sui-generis case of Diane de Maufrigneuse, Princesse de Cadignan, and the album she keeps. She is by now, following her separation from her husband and the Revolution of 1830, reduced to a life of economy and solitude in a simple apartment in the rue de Miromesnil, where she sees few friends, mainly the Marquise d'Espard, while looking out for a suitable wife for her son. The album is itself a precious object that she displays on a table in her salon: a gesture that no bourgeoise woman would dare. The album contains thirty portraits of "intimate friends" that society attributed to her as lovers. That, the narrator tells us, is a calumny, though at least ten of them authentically belong in the category. They are: Maxime de Trailles, elegant but sinister figure whom we knew as lover to Anastasie de Restaud and then about to be elected member from Arcis; Henri de Marsay, whom we have seen over and over again; Eugène de Rastignac, Victurnien d'Esgrignon, General Montriveau (the passionate would-be lover of Antoinette de Langeais); the Marquis de Ronquerolles, man of the world, one of The Thirteen along with Montriveau and de

Marsay; the Marquis d'Ajuda-Pinto, former lover of Claire de Beauséant, Rastignac's cousin and counsellor, whose apostasy caused her to leave Paris for her retreat in Normandy; the Prince Galathionne, a somewhat shady Russian; the young Ducs de Grandlieu and de Rhétoré, both representatives of Legitimist high society; the young Vicomte de Sérisy; and the "beautiful" Lucien de Rubempré. I count twelve. She calls the album the "anthology of her errors."

Only the aristocratic impertinence of the Faubourg Saint-Germain—believing itself exempt from the moral accountability of the bourgeoisie—could authorize the public display of the Princesse's album. But what strikes the reader who has made some progress across *The Human Comedy* is the rich impasto created by encountering these names. Even if some of them may be without much resonance (the Vicomte de Sérisy, for instance), most of them evoke whole narratives. Rastignac and Lucien, of course, and Montriveau—they are all principals in their own narratives, while reappearing in a number of others. Victurnien d'Esgrignon's liaison with Diane is the very crux of his financial problems and the fraud he commits, leading to his close encounter with justice, wherein Diane displays full loyalty to him but breaks off their love relationship. Someone like Miguel d'Adjuda-Pinto, of Portuguese origin, is less important, but his impending marriage to Berthe de Rochefide (other members of that family are important in several novels) triggers one of the main plot points of *Père Goriot* and sends us off to *The Abandoned Woman*, which recounts Claire de Beauséant's final attempt to find love with Gaston du Nueil. The name Grandlieu has wide resonance: Lucien attempts to marry the Duc's daughter Clotilde de

Grandlieu; we know this illustrious name is doomed to extinction since the Duc has nothing but daughters.

As Balzac's world becomes ever more crowded with his invented beings, there are temptations to catalogue them in quasi-Homeric fashion. In the preface to *A Daughter of Eve (Une Fille d'Eve)*, he suggests, facetiously but also in self-congratulation, the way an entry for one of his characters might look in a dictionary. He chooses Rastignac:

> Elder son of the Baron and Baroness de Rastignac, born at Rastignac in the Charente Department in 1799, comes to Paris in 1819 to study law, lives at the Pension Vauquer, where he meets Jacques Collin, aka Vautrin...[4]

And so on. Within the novels themselves, in addition to such social gatherings as that convened by Félicité des Touches, there is a very different moment in the story of the self-made perfume merchant, *César Birotteau (Histoire de la grandeur et de la décadence de César Birotteau)*. When he approaches the apogee of his rise in the world, with a new house newly furnished, César decides to give a grand ball, over the objections of his more prudent wife Constance. He proposes to make a list of invitees, with his daughter Césarine as scribe:

> "Very well, let's begin the list," said Birotteau, "with the upper crust. Césarine, write down: the Duc and Duchesse de Lenoncourt."
>
> "Heavens! César," said Constance, "don't send a single invitation to anyone you know merely as your client. Will you go invite the Princesse de Blamont-Chauvry, more closely related to your late godmother, the Marquise d'Uxelles, than the Duc de Leononcourt? Would you invite both Vandenesse brothers, M. de Marsay, M. de Ronquerolles, M. d'Aiglemont, that's to say all your clients? You're crazy, your success has turned your head."

"Yes, but the Comte de Fontaine and his family."

And it goes on:

"Take this down, Césarine. First, his honor the Prefect of the Seine. He'll come or not, but he is commander of the municipal corps: give merit where it is due! M. de la Billardière and his son, the mayor. Put the number of invitations at end of the list. My colleague M. Granet, second in command, and his wife. She's quite ugly, but it doesn't matter, we can't not invite her. M. Curel, the goldsmith, colonel in the National Guard, his wife and two daughters. Those are what I call 'the authorities.' Next the bigwigs! The Comte and Comtesse de Fontaine, and their daughter Emilie de Fontaine." (P 6: 162–3)

This goes on for three or four pages (depending or your edition); the list extends downward, to less exalted characters, some of whom will find it hard to know how to behave at the ball. It's fun for the experienced reader of Balzac—characters from other novels in *The Human Comedy* enter, if only as more or less implausible attendees at César's ball, each one sparking remembrance, or perhaps a kind of puzzled: where do I recall that name from? It's a game with aspects of an Agatha Christie novel but with a very different effect. The knowledge that you've heard of those people before, in different contexts, constitutes an intellectual exercise in world peopling. It brings a certain satisfaction if you can "place" most of them. It may, in the best of cases, provoke a curiosity about those you can't.

Excess

To his wife, César has succumbed to excess: he has lost a sense of his station in life and the manners that should reflect it. Excess is very much a theme that interests Balzac, and part of his very method of representation. It's integral to his attempt to say all. Excess proliferates throughout. In a world foreign to the honest César—who insists upon repaying every sou of the crushing debts that he accumulates, to die a figure of commercial probity—is the crowd of prostitutes of different sorts and degrees: *courtisanes, filles, lorettes, grisettes, rats d'opéra*, and other varieties that people Balzac's world, who incarnate excess, that of their clients and, as a result, of their own styles of life. There are more of these than would seem warranted in a reasonable census of the French population, as the critic Albert Béguin pointed out in his book on the visionary Balzac.[5] The prostitutes have, in Béguin's estimation, a special destiny, well explained by Etienne Lousteau in his tribute to the courtisane Esther, who has become Lucien's partner:

> At the age of eighteen, this girl has already known the greatest opulence, the most abject poverty, men at every social level. She holds a kind of magic wand with which she unleashes the brutal appetites so violently repressed in men who still have passions while working at politics or science, literature or art. There is no other woman in Paris who can say as she does to the Animal: "Outwith you!" And the Animal comes out of its cage and wallows in excess…"[6]

Esther is Circe, who turns Odysseus' men into swine: she understands and uses sex to release the demonic forces under the surface of social life. That might sound sinister but in Balzac's understanding it isn't necessarily: what Esther liberates is a fundamental, constitutive eros that proper society has too much hidden and repressed, and that demands its due. Sex in Balzac is dangerous but also animating. Esther, redeemed by her love for Lucien, becomes a sublime figure. When she realizes that she cannot escape Jacques Collin's sale of her to Nucingen, she self-consciously returns to the persona of the whore. She writes in a letter to her future possessor:

> I have never better understood the baseness of my condition than the day I was signed over to you. You have paid, I owe myself. There is nothing more sacred than the debts of dishonor. I don't have the right to *liquidate* myself by throwing myself into the Seine. One can always pay a debt in this frightful currency, which has value only on one of its sides: thus you will find me at your orders. I want to pay back in a single night all the sums that are mortgaged to this fatal moment, and I am certain that an hour of me is worth millions, all the more so that that this hour will be the last. Afterwards, I'll be even, and can take leave of life.   (P 6:603/P 197)

Esther's mordant wit and charm come through in this letter (which I don't cite in full); her pun on "liquidating" those debts of dishonor in the river points to her lucid intelligence about the role she has to play. She creates a salon that she fills with the cream of high prostitution, the dancers and actresses Tullia, Florentine, Fanny Beaupré, and Florine, and the notable Suzanne du Val-Noble, who join a group of distinguished and clever men, including Lousteau, Rastignac, Bixiou, Nathan, and others. Esther becomes "the most amusing, the most beautiful, the most elegant of the female Pariahs that compose the caste of kept women."

Esther offers the Baron her enduring friendship in place of sex, but that proposition of course goes nowhere. As she approaches the fatal night with Nucingen, we are told:

> she held in her heart an image of herself that at the same time made her blush and glorified her; the hour of her abdication was always present in her mind; thus she lived as if she were double, feeling pity for her persona....At once spectator and actor, judge and judged, she realized the admirable fiction of Arabian tales, where

you most often find a sublime being hidden within a degraded
envelope… (P6:643/P 239)

This doubleness constitutes what we might call a kind of irony,
that of the spectator at her own life who knows she is not at heart
what she must be for others. Esther, in addition to her designation
as the most beautiful of Balzac's women, is also one of the most
intelligent. She appears at the final dinner party that will end in
her bedding Nucingen dressed in virginal bridal white, to the
admiring exclamations of all. That irony comes to an end in the
early morning hours, when she takes the potent poison she has
kept for the occasion.

A version of this irony reappears when Suzanne du Val-Noble,
who has a long and illustrious career among Balzac's courtisanes,
plays host to the right-wing journalists who in *Lost Illusions* assemble in her apartment to sign the founding documents of the royalist newspaper *Le Réveil*. As she shows her guests the magnificence
of her apartment and its furnishings, she remarks: "Here are the
accounts of A Thousand and One Nights!"—"*Voilà les comptes des
Mille et une Nuits!*" (P5:493/ML 422). It's not easy to give a decent
translation of her pun: *comptes*, accounts, sounds like *contes*, stories; and *The Thousand and One Nights* is the most common French
title for *The Arabian Nights*. So Suzanne is saying that the wealth
and luxury of her surroundings derive from a thousand and one
nights of paid sex, and also that these nights are the source of as
many stories, like Scheherazade in *The Arabian Nights*, where stories are told to prolong desire, in order to evade the fate of the
Sultan's former partners, all doomed to execution at dawn. Sex
and storytelling stand in a dynamic mutual relation, of substitution and reinforcement. But the mediating factor, as Suzanne so

well understands and formulates in the concentrated form of the pun, is: money.

Balzac's courtisanes understand that love in the modern world is utterly tied to money: to luxury, including the furnishings of apartments made for love. It's not that Balzac invests all his understanding of love, or "love," in venal exchanges. In one of his prefaces he defends himself against accusations of immorality by making a list of all the "virtuous women" in *The Human Comedy*. There are appealing women and wives who remain faithful forever, so far as one can tell: Fanny Malvaut, discovered as a hardworking seamstress by the moneylender Gobseck, who becomes the lawyer Derville's beloved wife; Ursule Mirouët, virtuous despite persecution; the maltreated Pierrette Lorrain. Yet they tend to be most interesting when, like Henriette de Mortsauf in *The Lily of the Valley (Le lys dans la vallée)* their "virtue" is sorely tempted, their desires apparent under the bar of repression. Or like Antoinette de Langeais, in *The Duchesse de Langeais (La Duchesse de Langeais)* whose apparent virtue derives from ignorance more than innocence, and who once put in the way of discovering eros would wish to devote herself wholly to it. More to the point of Val-Noble's remark may be Rastignac's experience in discovering "Parisian love": that is to say love enveloped in luxury. It is simply more appealing than love in a garret, or love unadorned. The love of money and the love of eros are deeply conjoined in Balzac's world. Coralie's apartment before it is stripped of its luxury by bankruptcy, Suzanne du Val-Noble's apartment, the love nest that Old Goriot furnishes for his daughter Delphine de Nucingen's trysts with Rastignac: these are the places where love can feel most rewarding and rewarded. Excess in money and what it can buy matches well to sex unleashed.

Balzac in his late novel *Cousin Bette* (*La cousine Bette*) stages a meeting of suffering virtue and virtuous vice when Adeline Hulot, in search of her lecherous husband the Baron Hulot who has gone missing for two and a half years, visits Josépha Mirah, accomplished singer and one of the Baron's former kept women: she more or less cleaned him out and moved on to the Duc d'Hérouville. She is Jewish, like Esther, her name an anagram of Hiram: in the Balzacian imaginary, the most beautiful and passionate women seem to be mainly Jewish. She receives Adeline, whose own lodgings have been reduced to threadbare poverty by her husband's expenditures on Valérie Marneffe and other women, in the magnificence that her career has brought her:

> The luxury that in the past great lords displayed in their *petites maisons*, some of which remain still, "follies" that fully justify the name, stood out here with all the perfection of modern comforts, in the four rooms she could see, gently warmed by a stove with hidden vents.
>
> The Baroness, stupefied, examined each objet d'art with a profound astonishment. She was finding the explanation of how so many fortunes melted away in the crucible under which Pleasure and Vanity light an ardent fire.[7]

The scene between Adeline and Josépha—who has dressed herself with art and luxury—becomes a touching homage of "vice" to "virtue." The reader may well want to reverse the terms: Josépha is generous and grand (she has lent money to Hulot; she will send out tracers to find him and bring him to Adeline), Adeline largely pathetic. Virtue isn't in these circumstances much fun.

Adeline's wondering at how prostitutes and kept women consume fortunes echoes a moment of *A Harlot High and Low* where the narrator remarks that bourgeois wives cannot understand "how a fortune melts between the hands of these creatures whose social function, in the Fourierist system, is perhaps to make up for the sorrows caused by Avarice and Cupidity." (P 6:617/P 211).They might promote a kind of socialism. They belong to an economy that, as I suggested, is overheated. The healthy balance of income and expenditure is rare in Balzac, a well-regulated cash flow unheard of. The prostitutes represent one end of a spectrum of excess. As Aquilina puts it to Raphaël de Valentin at the orgy of *The Fatal Skin (La Peau de chagrin)*, Why should I worry about a future doesn't exist yet? She claims: "don't we live more in one day than a good bourgeoise lady does in ten years, and that says everything." (P 10: 116/S 70) When Raphaël signs on to the life of desire made possible by the magic skin, which grants every wish while shrinking as it does so, he becomes a spender like Aquilina and her ilk, devoted to the life of debauch and its technicolor pleasures. When he realizes that an existence under the aegis of desire swiftly brings death into view as its end, he tries to arrest forward movement, to create the stasis of a life without desire. In vain. He is merely living in a parabolic mode the fate of all human creatures. He incarnates excess.

The Human Comedy features a sharp division of spenders and savers. At the other end of the spectrum from the life of excess are such as the usurer Gobseck or the antiques dealer of *The Fatal Skin*, who has reached the age of 102 by refusing to spend, enjoying his pleasures uniquely in his mind, in what he calls knowledge as opposed to the dynamic of wanting and having that characterizes most of humankind. Gobseck sits unmoving in his room while all the passions of Paris come to play themselves out before his eyes—since all passions require money. If some of Balzac's young heroes live the life of saving at first—Raphaël shivers in a cold garret room, writing a treatise on the will; Félix de Vandenesse is deprived of all love, pleasure, and spending money; Louis Lambert suffers as the scapegoat in his school—this is usually from necessity rather than choice. Once the chance comes, they will join the spenders. Lucien is again a case in point: once poetry has been abandoned in favor of journalism, he becomes a *viveur*, one of those young people who doesn't think about the morrow. In his case, the only outcome he can think of is suicide—but then Jacques Collin/Vautrin/Carlos Herrera arrives on the scene to propose another dénouement, with Lucien become his creature, the vehicle of his vicarious enjoyment of the world.

Savers and spenders are defined not only by their uses of money but as well by their uses of sex. The two come to be virtually indistinguishable. The problem is almost always posed in terms of male sexuality: the male has only a limited supply of sperm, which he can spend profligately or save up, repressing the need for expenditure. ("Spending" as a traditional term for orgasm suggests a large societal investment in the equivalent of money and sperm.[8]) Again, Raphaël's experience with his magic talisman gives the most overt form of the problem: after the granting of each wish, the magic skin shrivels (like the penis). Eventually, it will be as small as the petal of a flower as Raphaël's beloved Pauline holds it in the palm of her hand; and in her lover's final paroxysm of desire she will feel it tickle her hand as it shrinks to nothing. Death comes as the bankruptcy of desire. If this is the problem of the young, though most don't see it with the lucidity the talisman provides to Raphaël, the old savers are more problematic. What they have gained through their renunciation of desire ought to be some kind of wisdom that allows them to understand the decisive forces of existence, as the antiques' dealer claims to do, as Gobseck seems really to do. Yet the antiques' dealer is at the last undone by the very talisman he gives Raphaël, since Raphaël wishes that the old man fall in love with a dancer, and we later see him haggard and infatuated with a prostitute. And Gobseck dies surrounded by rotting goods for which in his dotage he hasn't been able to negotiate trades. And there are those who seem to have sexualized thought itself, in the manner that Freud suggests intellectuals do: the *Wisstrieb* or epistemophilic instinct becomes invested in thinking. That's the case of Balthasar Claës in *The Search for the Absolute* and possibly the painter Frenhofer in *The Unknown Masterpiece* and certainly the philosopher Louis Lambert, who is about to trade the sexualized mind for sex with his wife to be, Pauline de Villenoix, and then on the eve of his wedding tries to castrate himself. And then sinks into madness. It's as if he couldn't have it both ways.

The sex/money problematic ramifies in many ways: gambling, which obsesses many a Balzacian young man, appears a kind of masturbation, leading to sheer loss (rarely gain), as in the scene at the start of *The Fatal Skin* where Raphaël, reduced to his last twenty-franc piece, goes to the gambling dens of the Palais-Royal for a last effort to redeem his fortunes, loses, then heads for the banks of the Seine. It's while waiting for nightfall to cover his suicide that he discovers the antiques shop and the magic skin that will provide him with what the antiques' dealer calls a postponed suicide. For the women of *The Human Comedy* the issues are evidently more complicated. Yet for Henriette de Mortsauf who over the years represses the intense desires that Félix's kisses have awakened in her, the result is dying from thirst and inanition: repression seems no healthier than expenditure. Hélène d'Aiglemont of

The Woman of Thirty clearly finds sexual fulfillment with the criminal-become-pirate she elopes with—but it is not lasting, and she dies stripped of all worldly goods. That panther of *A Passion in the Desert* may be the most robustly happy of Balzac's female inventions but she will have to die at her lover's hand through a "misunderstanding."

"Desire sets us afire and power destroys us," the antiques' dealer tells Raphaël, and *The Human Comedy* doesn't propose any way out, no doubt because there isn't one. The economy described and created by Balzac heads toward inevitable entropy, by way of ecstatic outbursts of energy. It's clear that Balzac intended to see *The Fatal Skin* as exemplary of and for his time. When it was reprinted in 1832 (the first edition sold out quickly) in his collection called *Romans et Contes philosophiques*, it carried an Introduction signed by Philarète Chasles, a close friend of Balzac's who was voicing the novelist's view of his own work, in fact possibly writing under Balzac's dictation. Chasles sees the lesson of the novel as one about modern egotism and its destructiveness for social cohesion. He writes of Raphaël:

> Under the command of his terrible talisman, he lives and dies in a convulsion of egotism. It's this individualism (*personnalité*) that twists the heart and devours the innards of the society in which we live. The more it increases, the more individuals become isolated; no more ties to one another, no more life in common. Individualism reigns; it's its triumph and rage that *The Fatal Skin* has reproduced. In this book, there is the whole of our time.[9]

The plaint of the political and social reactionary who looks back with nostalgia on an Ancien Régime that was supposedly a time of an organic, harmonious society, with the common good placed above the individual's demands.

The Melodramatic Mode

But if *The Fatal Skin* claims representative, exemplary value as a picture of contemporary France, we have to come to terms with Balzac's understanding of representation. *The Fatal Skin* may be a parabolic instance, as he recognizes, "philosophical" in its wish to go behind social façades to the forces moving society. But all his works, including those most attached to representing social realities, share the hyperbolic terms of representation that are in full flower in this first grandly successful novel of his. I come back at the end, with a certain inevitability, to where I began in my thinking about Balzac: his excess, his melodramatic terms of representation, which pushed me to writing *The Melodramatic Imagination*.[10] I tried in that book to show the continuing validity of melodrama as an imaginative mode and form of representation, extending forward to such as Henry James and Joseph Conrad and William Faulkner, and, I thought, rooted in stage melodrama that came to the fore during the French Revolution, with the decline of classical tragedy. The melodramatic mode seeks to make visible the large stakes of existence, to articulate the fundamental imperatives of the drama—those, usually, of how people violate the freedom of others. It's very much a form for the dawning age of individualism and democratic representational arts. It affirms the right to happiness of the oppressed, it punishes tyrants, it makes available to all the home truths of ethical life. Such subtle novelists as James transmute its overt terms into a melodrama of consciousness, one in which the stakes remain tremendous, the violation of others' inwardness the stuff of lurid crime.

Balzac's social representations all tend to the melodramatic, as how could they not given his totalizing ambitions. Examples are not far to seek, and the interested reader can find a number of them in *The Melodramatic Imagination*. Let me here give a different example, from Balzac's late novel *Cousin Bette* where a certain irony threads through the initial scene of the novel, yet an irony that may only heighten the stakes of the encounter, make them more visible, and their future more ominous. The lateness of this novel in Balzac's work layers melodrama and satire in a self-conscious enactment of the Balzacian method itself. The novel opens with the visit of Célestin Crevel, former *parfumeur,* successor to César Birotteau as owner of *La Reine des Roses*, now wealthy, possessor of the Légion d'Honneur and captain in the National Guard—he likes to wear his uniform—to Adeline Hulot, the neglected wife of the high functionary Baron Hector Hulot d'Ervy. Crevel's daughter is married to the Hulot's son. Now Adeline needs a dowry for her own daughter, Hortense, which her husband is unable to provide since he has wasted a fortune on his concubines. Crevel, who is enraged that Hulot lured away his own mistress, Josépha, has a plan that ought both to satisfy his desire for vengeance on the Baron and his own lust for Adeline: if she gives in to his advances, he'll provide Hortense's dowry.

Crevel's approach to seduction is not subtle. The scene allows Balzac at once to satirize the man and his inept address to Adeline, to allow melodrama to unfold its emotional satisfactions, and to parody Crevel's and possibly his own melodramatic stagings. Crevel is on his knees before Adeline:

"You do see it: you're unhappy.

"I, Monsieur?

"Yes, beautiful and noble creature!" exclaimed Crevel, "you have suffered so very much…"

"Monsieur, end this talk and leave! Or else speak to me properly."

"Do you know, Madame, how your Hulot and I became acquainted? Through our mistresses, Madame."

"Oh, Monsieur…"

"Through our mistresses, Madame," repeated Crevel in a melodramatic voice, shifting his position in order to gesture with his right hand.

"Very well, so? Monsieur," the Baronne said quietly, to the great astonishment of Crevel.

Seducers with petty motives never understand great souls.

(P 7:63/ML 11–12)

Crevel now tells the story of how after the death of his wife he did not want to remarry in the interest of maintaining the family fortune, destined to go to his daughter, so instead took up with a fifteen-year-old working girl of a "miraculous beauty" (the same Josépha Adeline will encounter hundreds of pages later), an arrangement presented as the practical bourgeois's solution to love, sex, and keeping inheritances intact. (One may hear an echo of Crevel's solution in the first sentence of J. M. Coetzee's *Disgrace:* "For a man of his age, fifty-two, divorced, he has, to his mind, solved the problem of sex rather well."[11]) Hulot, who himself has been "protecting" a young actress, steals Josépha from Crevel, destroying his happiness. In compensation for her husband's treachery to him, Crevel tells Adeline, she must become his mistress.

Madame Hulot looked at this calculating bourgeois with a glance fixed by terror; he thought she might have gone mad, and stopped for a moment. "It's you who made it happen, you covered me with scorn, you defied me, and I spoke!" he said, seeing the need to justify the brutality of his last words.

"My daughter, my daughter!" exclaimed the Baroness in the voice of despair.

"Ah, I have lost my senses!" Crevel went on. "The day Josépha was taken from me I was like a tigress who's had her cubs taken from her....Really I was just the way I see you now. Your daughter! She's now for me the means of having you. Yes, I sabotaged her marriage. And you won't be able to marry her without my help! However beautiful Mademoiselle Hortense may be, she needs a dowry."

"Alas, yes," said the Baronne, wiping away her tears.

"So just try asking the Baron for ten thousand francs," said Crevel, resuming his position.

He paused for a moment, like an actor waiting for applause.

(7: 67–8/ ML 16–17)

And then he goes on: the Baron will put her in the poorhouse in order to pursue his sexual pleasures.

"You are already well on the way to the workhouse. Look, in the years since I was last here you haven't renovated any of the furnishings of your salon. The word WANT is spewed forth by all the rips and rears of these fabrics. Who is the son-in-law who wouldn't leave terrified by the ill-disguised evidence of the most horrible of poverties, that of people of fashion? I have been a shopkeeper, I know whereof I speak. There's nothing like the eye of the Paris tradesman for distinguishing real riches from merely apparent riches....You haven't a sou left," he said, lowering his voice. "You see it everywhere, even in your servant's livery. Do you want me to reveal horrible mysteries concealed from you?"

"Monsieur," said Madame Hulot, who was crying into her tear-soaked handkerchief, "That's enough, enough!"

"Well then! My son-in-law gives money to his father. That's what I wanted to tell you at the outset, about how your son is carrying on. But I have been keeping an eye on my daughter's interests, don't you worry."

"Oh! To marry off my daughter and then die!" cried the unfortunate woman... (P 7: 68/ML 17)

The melodrama of this scene is complex in its nature and opera-tions. Its sublimity is undercut by Crevel's awareness of himself as acting a part—yet it's a part he can't not act, he is driven by lust for Adeline and vengeful rage against her husband. The wholly bour-geois issues at stake—Hortense's dowry, Crevel's savings for his daughter, the shabby state of the Hulot furniture—make sublim-ity difficult. And overarching the scene is the narrator's awareness of how sordid Crevel is, how far from the operatic lover that he'd like to be (that Josépha becomes a great lyric artist hovers some-where in the background). Balzac's use of melodrama here is ironic: neither the theme nor the actors can truly claim the glorious articu-lations and enactments of melodrama. And yet: Adeline surely is driven into a fully melodramatic situation, given a choice between her own dishonor or that of her daughter's lifelong spinsterhood. By the time she cries out: "Oh! To marry off my daughter and then die!" she has achieved true melodramatic resonance. And earned it: she has attained a position where the stakes of her life are starkly clear, and her fate stands written before her.

These introductory pages of *Cousin Bette* are brilliant in laying out the future arc of the plot, which Crevel in general terms has understood well enough: Hulot's manic, driven philandering will destroy the family, lead Hulot to fraud and crime, causing the suicide of his respectable uncle Johann Fischer. It doesn't, though, tell of the entry on the stage of the title character, the poor and vengeful Hulot cousin Lisbeth Fischer, and the woman who will become her ally in the destruction of the Hulot household, the beautiful and utterly venal and nasty Valérie Marneffe. I used to think *Cousin Bette* almost decadent among Balzac novels, a kind of final fling into which he tosses everything in his arsenal, including an exotic tropical disease brought by Valérie's favorite lover, the Brazilian Montès de Montéjanos, that will kill her off when she has married Crevel. There is a bit too much in this novel, too many tricks from the well-stocked storehouse of earlier novels. And there is too much of Bette and Valérie and vengeances beyond measure. But it also, I now think, shows Balzac in full mastery of the techniques he had been trying out since his youthful excursions into the Gothic novel (published under pseudonyms): his repertory of melodramatic means of representation is not only on full display, it is often accompanied by a kind of self-awareness about the uses and effects of melodramatic imagination.

Much later in *Cousin Bette,* Valérie Marneffe learns that Adeline has herself summoned Crevel and offered him sweet words in the attempt to get 200,000 francs she needs to bail out Johann Fischer. When she hears the words "Hulot" and "200,000 francs," Valérie turns to Crevel with "a glance that shot, like the glint of a cannon in the smoke of battle, through her long eyelashes." (P 7:333/ML 310) She asks Crevel: "What did she do to strike pity in you, that old woman! What part of herself did she show you—her religion?" When Crevel calls Adeline "saintly," Valérie goes into an act demonstrating her own piety: she claims to recall her first communion, her remorse at having become an adulteress, her deep respect for all that is religious, her fear of God's justice; she evokes her patron Sainte Valérie, and decides she must return to the side of her husband, the ailing Monsieur Marneffe. She says a final farewell to Crevel, who now is in tears. And then:

> "You big dolt," she exclaimed, with an infernal blast of laughter, "that's the way pious women go about extracting a wad of two hundred thousand francs from you!" (P 7:335/ML 313)

Valérie mocks the melodrama at the heart of Adeline's hard existence. And in doing so achieves the goal of preventing Crevel from becoming Adeline's benefactor. Melodrama, it seems, has become a malleable tool that cannot be counted upon to preserve its traditional reference to a polarized vice and virtue.

Reading

Reading Balzac. There is an arresting moment of direct address to the reader on page two of *Père Goriot*, after the narrator has evoked the car of Juggernaut crushing hearts and continuing its route unabated.

> So will you do, you who hold this book in your white hand, you who sink into a comfortable armchair while telling yourself: "Maybe this book will amuse me." After having read the secret griefs of Père Goriot, you will dine with a good appetite while attributing your insensitivity to the author, claiming he exaggerates, writes fantasies. Ah! but know this: this drama is neither a fiction nor a novel. *All is true*; it is so accurate that anyone can recognize its elements at home, in their heart perhaps.   (P 3:50/S 6)

This is a bit inept, something like the melodramatic actor striking the boards with his heel to underline an important utterance. Yet it also suggests the somewhat contradictory task of the novelist, and Balzac's particular aim for his novels. They must amuse the upper classes, those with white hands, exempt from manual labor, protected by kid gloves from the elements. That white hand may well be a woman's; we have noted Balzac's popularity with women readers. The novelist must amuse, entertain those who sit in soft armchairs, and who dine well. And yet: he wants to make a difference, to upset you as well as entertain you. The claim that his novel is not one, not romance but reality, is by Balzac's time an old one. But he gives it a special turn of the screw. His *All is true*—in English in the text—strains to make the point that a novel can tell of reality even while amusing.[12] Its heightened reality can be given a local habitation—and recognized in the heart by those willing to do so.

There weren't many existing models for the kind of novel Balzac wished to write: Walter Scott was the best, but he wrote about times long past. Balzac wanted to do the history of the nearly contemporary moment. How to succeed in that task? He needed to please, even to seduce—that white hand had to keep turning pages. But he wanted to make the case for hard social realities unknown to those in comfortable armchairs. Yet if these realities needed careful presentation, description and analysis, on some level, the emotional and psychological let's say, they could be recognized in the reader's heart because they are not limited by caste distinctions. They are everywhere.

So the ideal reader of Balzac should relax in a comfortable chair, ready to be entertained, yet also alert to the possibility of drama that may change the way she or he thinks about the world. Henry James insisted that Balzac was "the father of us all"—all novelists. That has puzzled many readers and critics who take their stand within the tradition of the more decorous and reticent English novel. I think we need to take James's estimate seriously: it's Balzac who invented the serious novel of social life, the novel that entertains but also takes as its goal making us see through other eyes, into other houses and lives, loves and obsessions. Balzac's protean creation of character—there are over 2,400 fictional persons in *The Human Comedy*—speaks to his need to enter the bodies and minds of others, to extend the single life by way of myriad others. To know the world as it is means using fictions, imagining what it is like to be someone else in that person's circumstances and dilemmas, telling the story of how circumstances and dilemmas came to be, making clear their stakes, conjuring the large forces that necessitated them. Making of it all a heightened drama in which the choices and gambles of life become evident, are enacted and articulated before us. And at the same making sure that his novels are not mere pastimes. All is true.

Recently, I found in a derelict looking file cabinet—ready for the Pension Vauquer?—some notes that must date from around 1985, notes for the next book I would write after *Reading for the Plot* (1984). It was to be on Balzac. It never was written; it took me over thirty years to return to Balzac (I had to be sure evoked him in essays and chapters) and to figure out how to write a book about him. My first effort was *Balzac's Lives,* published in 2020, where I undertook to write the biographies of some of Balzac's 2,472 fictional characters.[13] It had dawned on me that some account of Balzac's extraordinary creation of imaginary persons might be a way to suggest the pleasures and the stakes of reading *The Human Comedy.* His creation of fictional lives must best even Shakespeare's. What does it mean? How do we as readers respond to this proliferation of characters?

The substance of the book: all these invented people, in their origins, their careers, their ambitions, their loves, their successes and failures, especially in their interactions, together represent a vast panorama of life as it was lived at a moment of rapid social transformation, in the wake of the French Revolution and the Napoleonic epic. Balzac gives us the dynamics of a society in early capitalist development, where old systems of social cohesion have been lost, where everything seems to be up for grabs, where individual ambition may lead to fortune but lays bare the shredding of the social fabric. Balzac's ambitious young men—there are some women too—remain extraordinarily close to us because they insistently ask: who are we, individually and as a collectivity? How do you know who people are, what to expect from them and how to evaluate them, in this new social order where everyone wears black, where the clear signs of social distinction of the Old Régime have vanished? There are vertiginous new freedoms, opportunities for self-definition, for the "self-made man," but in Balzac's view at tremendous cost. Individualism reigns, and it's exciting—but the result is an unstable social order. The great question in Balzac's world becomes: who are you? What can I know about you? Can I trust you? The world he grasps and represents is undoubtedly a first sketch of our own world. He ushers us into modernity.

Beyond that: the act of Balzacian creation itself gives us some insight into our reading of novels, of what we seek in them and love about them. We spend time and energy and emotion with persons who never existed, we invest affect into them, we carry on dialogues with them, they come to incarnate for us different ways of being in the world, different optics on reality. Balzac's profligate creation and his use of returning characters from one novel to the next lets us understand, better than almost any other novelist, why the novel has become the dominant genre of our modernity. It's in the novel that we work out the problems of our selves and the social structures that we must learn to deal with, to protest against as well.

Balzac's excess, his ready recourse to melodramatic representation, probably harmed him in the eyes of readers brought up on high modernism. Despite Henry James's life-long fidelity to Balzac, his repeated claim that any true novelist must learn the lesson of Balzac, James's progeny in the novel and in criticism have largely ignored Balzac. In France, he remains a national monument, taught in schools, put on national exams, available in many paperback editions. In the English-speaking world, it is hard to find new translations of all but the best-known works—whereas if you go back to around 1900, there were competing English translations of the whole of the *Human Comedy* on the market. Some of my hesitation and delay in writing about Balzac was motivated by the sense that he had no more traction in the U.S. and the U.K. And yet: didn't "postmodernism," with its new indulgence of ornament, excess, and violations of classical proportion, seem to open the way for a return of Balzac? That's been my hope and my argument.

So now after the years of postponement I have published two books on Balzac—this the second, and the one in which the format has allowed me to talk about my personal experience as a reader of his novels. That experience, to be fully honest in these final paragraphs, has been fitful, disorganized, incomplete. I never set out to read the whole of *The Human Comedy*—it's perhaps my idiosyncrasy that I would have found such an ambition and enterprise too daunting to be accomplished. Instead, I have picked up a novel here and a tale there when the Balzac urge has come upon me. My Balzac canon expanded only gradually, then more recently, with the determination to write about him, picked up speed and led me to works I had neglected: either never read, or read earlier on without much appreciation. So it was with *A Murky Business,* as I mentioned already: I have now promoted it to the list of my favorites. *The Old Maid* and *The Collection of Antiquities* had long put me off by their very titles, which do seem inadequate to the dramas they stage once you overcome your standoffishness and plunge in.

My reading of Balzac has been a gradual filling in of outlines, and at the same time a relaxation of critical strictures—allowing myself to fall under the spell of what by the standards taught by the English novel or the French novel in the wake of Flaubert seemed less than high art. Balzac in France has always suffered from the reputation of not "writing well," with a regard for the decorum of French prose. True enough, but Balzacian prose at its most intense takes us somewhere else, promotes our ambitions to understand and conquer in simulation of his characters: to grasp everything, to understand how each person and situation and lodging and accessory is related to all others. In reading Balzac we at moments achieve a kind of vision of the world as "will and idea," to use Schopenhauer's terms: as a potential totality that we might almost be able to understand and master. It's a visionary enterprise. It works only when we as readers allow ourselves to enter a visionary mode, to respond to the staginess of enactments, to seize the high stakes of the drama, to accept the premises of melodrama. To a potential reader of Balzac the response of this reader is most of all: don't hold back. Work with the terms of representation you are given, submit to the manic summons to enter this invented world so much more legible than ours, and to deal with the excessive appetites of these persons. Then you will find yourself wanting more; and find more to satisfy you. Henry James, once again, in conclusion: "What it comes back to, in other words, is the intensity with which we live—and his intensity is recorded for us on every page of his work."

ACKNOWLEDGMENTS

L et me first thank Anne Cheng who, along with Philip Davis, Marina Warner, and Michael Wood, asked me to contribute to the *My Reading* series and responded generously to my proposed book; all four of them have supported my effort ever since. Some parts of my text reflect earlier publication in journals, with my thanks to Arien Mack and Francesco Spandri. Then thanks to some friends and colleagues with whom I have dialogued about Balzac over the years, in particular: D. A. Miller, Rachel Bowlby, Susannah Lee, Claudie Bernard, Martine Reid, Mariolina Bertini, Paolo Tortonese, Janet Beizer, Rebecca Sugden, Edwin Frank. And my thanks for the graceful editorial direction of Jacqueline Norton.

FURTHER READING

A few novels by Balzac:

In French, just about every title of *La Comédie humaine* is available in paperback, either Folio or Garnier/Flammarion. A few recommendations for great reads available in English translation:

Père Goriot, trans. Henry Reed. Signet Classics.

The Fatal Skin, trans. Atwood H. Townsend. Signet Classics

Lost Illusions, trans. Kathleen Raine. Modern Library.

Lost Souls, trans. Raymond MacKenzie. University of Minnesota Press. [The older and better-known translation by Rayner Heppenstall, published by Penguin, titles the novel *A Harlot High and Low*; I have referred to that throughout my book; I think the new MacKenzie translation is better despite the somewhat aberrant title.]

A Murky Business, trans. Herbert J. Hunt. Penguin.

Cousin Bette, trans. Kathleen Raine. Modern Library.

The Human Comedy: Selected Stories, ed. Peter Brooks. New York Review Books.

Biographies of Balzac:

David A. Carter, *Brief Lives: Balzac*. Hesperus.

V. S. Pritchett, *Balzac*. Alfred A. Knopf.

Graham Robb, *Balzac*. Picador.

Stefan Zweig, *Balzac*. Viking Press.

Critical Studies:

Balzac, *Père Goriot*, trans. Burton Raffel, ed. Peter Brooks (this Norton Critical Edition of the novel contains a selection of classic and modern essays on Balzac). Norton.

Roland Barthes, *S/Z.*, trans. Richard Miller. Hill and Wang.

Janet L. Beizer, *Balzac's Narrative Generations*. Yale University Press.

Peter Brooks, *Balzac's Lives*. New York Review Books.

Michel Butor, "Balzac and Reality," trans. Remy Hall, in *Inventory*, trans., ed. Richard Howard. Jonathan Cape.

Owen Heathcote and Andrew Watts, *The Cambridge Companion to Balzac*. Cambridge University Press.

Henry James, "The Lesson of Balzac," in *Literary Criticism*, vol. 2. Library of America.

Harry Levin, "Balzac," in *The Gates of Horn*. Oxford University Press.

Michael Lucey, *The Misfit of the Family: Balzac and the Social Forms of Sexuality*. Duke University Press.

Georg Lukacs, *Studies in European Realism*, trans. Edith Bone. Merlin Press.

Anthony Pugh, *Balzac's Recurring Characters*. University of Toronto Press.

Only available in French:

André Allemand, *Unité et structure de l'univers balzacien*. Plon.

Maurice Bardèche, *Balzac romancier*. Plon.

Albert Béguin, *Balzac visionnaire*, reprinted in *Balzac lu et relu*. Editions du Seuil.

Jean-Louis Bory, *Pour Balzac et quelques autres*. Juillard.

Gérard Gengembre, *Balzac: le forçat des lettres*. Perrin.

Fernand Lotte, *Dictonnaire biographique des personnages fictifs de la Comédie humaine*. Corti.

Pierre Michon, *Trois auteurs*. Verdier.

Nicole Mozet, *Balzac au pluriel*. Presses Universitaires de France.

NOTES

Chapter 1

1. The work of mine I refer to is *The Novel of Worldliness* (Princeton: Princeton University Press, 1969).
2. See Oscar Wilde, "The Decay of Lying," in *Intentions and Other Writings* (Garden City, NY: Dolphin Books, 1981), 34.
3. Honoré de Balzac, *Le Père Goriot* in *La comédie humaine* (12 vols. Paris: Bibliothèque de la Pléiade, 1976) 3:54; English trans. Henry Reed, *Père Goriot* (New York: Signet, 2004), 10. I will continue to give references to these editions, henceforth within parentheses in the text. Translations will be my own, though I have consulted the existing translations and borrowed from them more or less, depending on how close they remain to the original.
4. See Balzac's preface to *A Daughter of Eve (Une fille d'Eve)*, Pléiade 2: 265–6.
5. See Roland Barthes, *S/Z* (Paris: Editions du Seuil, 1970); English trans. Richard Miller (New York: Hill and Wang, 1975).
6. Henry James, Preface to *The American* in *Literary Criticism* (2 vols. New York: Library of America, 1984), 2:1064.
7. Balzac, *Illusions perdues*, Pléiade 5:708. English trans. Kathleen Raine, *Lost Illusions* (New York: Modern Library, 2001), 670.
8. Balzac, *La Maison Nucingen*, Pléiade 6:332. English trans. Katherine Prescott Wormeley, *Nucingen and Co., Bankers* in *La Comédie Humaine of Honoré de Balzac* (Boston: Little, Brown, 1901), vol. 15.

Chapter 2

1. See Marcel Proust, *Contre Sainte-Beuve*, ed. Pierre Clarac (Paris: Bibliothèque de la Pléiade, 1971), 277.
2. *A Passion in the Desert*, trans. Carol Cosman, in Honoré de Balzac, *The Human Comedy: Selected Stories*, ed. Peter Brooks (New York: New York Review Books, 2014), 142 / *Une Passion dans le désert*, Pléiade 8:1219. It's not irrelevant to the story that Monsieur Martin was reputed to make

his animals docile by masturbating them. For an extended discussion of the tale, see Janet L. Beizer, *Family Plots: Balzac's Narrative Generations* (New Haven: Yale University Press, 1986).

3. *La Fille aux yeux d'or*, Pléiade 5: 1092; English trans. Peter Collier, *The Girl with the Golden Eyes* (Oxford: Oxford World Classics, 2012), 120.

4. See on Balzac's woman readership, Marcel Bouteron, *Lettres de femmes adressées à H. de Balzac (1837–1840)*, in *Cahiers Balzaciens*, nos. 3 and 5 (Paris: La Cité des Livres, 1924–27); and David Bellos, "Reconnaissances: Balzac et son public féminin," *Oeuvres critiques* 9, no. 3 (1985); and Christiane Mounoud-Anglés, *Balzac et ses lectrices* (Paris: Indigo et Côté Femmes Editions, 1994).

5. Charles Augustin Sainte-Beuve, "M. de Balzac," *Revue des Deux-Mondes*, November 15, 1834.

6. *Une ténébreuse affaire*, Pléiade 8: 537–8; English trans. Herbert J. Hunt, *A Murky Business* (Harmondsworth, UK: Penguin, 1972), 59.

7. On Delacroix's "moments," see Peter Brooks, *History Painting and Narrative: Delacroix's Moments* (Oxford: Legenda, 1998); for Sartre's perfect moments, see *La Nausée* (1938; Paris: Livre de Poche, 1957), 92.

8. Pierre Corneille, *Cinna, ou la clémence d'Auguste* (1640), V, 3, 1697–8.

9. *Cinna*, V, 3, 1696–7.

10. *La Femme de trente ans*, Pléiade 2: 1113–14; English trans. Ellen Marriage, *A Woman of Thirty* (New York: Macmillan, 1901).

11. *Le Lys dans la vallée*, Pléiade 9:1215; English trans. Luciennne Hill (New York: Carroll and Graf, 1989), 242.

Chapter 3

1. Balzac, Préface to *Illusions perdues*, part 3, Pléiade 5:120. For Lukács, see his "Illusions perdues," in *Balzac et le réalisme français*, trans. Paul Lavau (Paris: Maspéro, 1967).

2. Balzac, "Préface" to *Illusions perdues*, part 3, Pléiade 5:121.

3. Alceste Chapuys-Montlaville, in Lise Dumasy, ed. *La Querelle du roman-feuilleton. Littérature, presse et politique, un débat précurseur (1836–1848)*. Grenoble: ELLUG, Université Stendhal, 1999, 99.

4. Dumasy, 100.

5. Dumasy, 108.

6. *Illusions perdues*, Pléiade 5:403; English trans. Kathleen Raine, *Lost Ilusions* (New York: Modern Library, 2001), 318.

7. *La Peau de chagrin*, Pléiade 10:93; English trans. Atwood Townsend, *The Fatal Skin* (New York: Signet), 45.

8. "*Sarrasine* represents the very trouble of representation, the uncontrolled (pandemic) circulation of signs, of sexes, and of fortunes." Roland Barthes, *S/Z* (Paris: Editions du Seuil, 1970), 230; English trans. Richard Miller, *S/Z* (New York: Hill and Wang, 1975), 216.

9. Balzac, *Ferragus* in *Histoire des Treize*, Pléiade 5:793; English trans. Herbert J. Hunt, *History of the Thirteen* (Harmondsworth: Penguin, 1974), 31.

10. Pierre Rosanvallon, *Le Peuple introuvable. Histoire de la représentation démocratique en France* (Paris: Gallimard, 1998), 288.

11. See, for instance, the classic study by Louis Chevalier, *Classes laborieuses et classes dangereuses* (Paris: Plon, 1958); English trans, Frank Jellinek, *Labouring Classes and Dangerous Classes* (London: Routledge and Kegan Paul, 1973), which ranges freely across Balzac's work for sociological insight.

12. *Autre étude de femme*, Pléiade 3:691; English trans. Jordan Stump in *The Human Comedy: Selected Stories* (New York: New York Review Books, 2014), 36.

13. See Walter Benjamin, "The Storyteller" [Der Erzähler] in *The Storyteller Essays*, trans. Tess Lewis, ed. Samuel Titan (New York: New York Review Books, 2019), 52.

14. See Michel Jeanneret, *Des mets et des mots* (Paris: José Corti, 1987).

15. On the complicated prehistory of *Olympia*—doubtless Balzac's own parody—see Mariolina Bertini, "Du Théâtre au roman: 'l'Olympia' de Balzac," in *L'Année balzacienne*, no. 13 (2012), 267–93.

Chapter 4

1. The title of the English translation currently available is: *The Seamy Side of History*. Not accurate.

2. See Balzac, *Gobseck*, Pléiade 2:983; English trans. Linda Asher, *Gobseck*, in Honoré de Balzac, *The Human Comedy: Selected Stories*, 249.

3. Thomas Piketty, *Capital in the Twenty-First Century*, trans. Arthur Goldhammer (Cambridge: Harvard University Press, 2014), 207 ff.

4. Balzac, *Le Député d'Arcis*, Pléiade 8:736; English trans. Ellen Marriage, *The Member for Arcis*, in *The Works of Honore de Balzac* (New York & Chicago: E.R. Dumont, 1901), 37: 24.

5. Stendhal, *Lucien Leuwen*, in *Romans et Nouvelles* (2 vols. Paris: Bibliothèque de la Pléiade, 1963), 1:1234.

6. Erich Auerbach, *Mimesis*, trans. Willard Trask (Princeton: Princeton University Press, 1953. See chapter 18, "In the Hôtel de la Mole."

7. Balzac, *Le Cabinet des Antiques*, Pléiade 4:1054; English trans. Ellen Marriage, *The Collection of Antiquities* (Project Gutenberg reprint, 2010), 216–17.

8. See *Du Droit d'aînesse*, par M. D*** (Paris: Delongchamps, Dentu, Petit, 1824).

9. Balzac, *Sarrasine*, P 6:1046; English trans. Jordan Stump, *Sarrasine*, in *The Human Comedy: Short Stories*, 112.

10. Karl Marx, *The Communist Manifesto*, ed. Jeffrey C. Isaac (New Haven: Yale University Press, 2012), 77.

11. Balzac, *Splendeurs et misères des courtisanes*, Pléiade 6:923; English trans. Rayner Heppenstall, *A Harlot High and Low* (London: Penguin, 1970), 541. A new and better translation by Raymond MacKenzie is now available, under the odd title *Lost Souls* (Minneapolis: University of Minnesota Press, 2021).

12. Balzac, *Gobseck*, Pléiade 2:969; *Gobseck*, in *The Human Comedy: Selected Stories*, 233.

13. Oscar Wilde, "The Decay of Lying," in *Intentions and Other Writings* (Garden City, NY: Dolphin Books, 1981), 34.

14. Marcel Proust, *A la recherche du temps perdu* (4 vols. Paris: Bibliothèque de la Pléiade, 4:621; English trans. Andreas Mayor and Terence Kilmartin, revised by D. J. Enright, *In Search of Lost Time: Time Regained* (New York: Modern Library, 2003), 526.

15. Henry James, "The Lesson of Balzac," in *Literary Criticism* (2 vols. New York: Library of America, 1984), 2: 136.

Chapter 5

1. See my *Troubling Confessions: Speaking Guilt in Law and Literature* (Chicago: University of Chicago Press, 2000).

2. J.-J. Rousseau, *Confessions, Autres textes autobiographiques* (Paris: Bibliothèque de la Pléiade, 1962), 175; English trans. Angela Scholar, *Confessions* (Oxford: Oxford World Classics, 2000), 170.

3. *Confessions*, Pléiade 59–60; Oxford 58.

4. Balzac, Préface to *Une fille d'Eve*, Pléiade 3:265.

5. Albert Béguin, *Balzac visionnaire* (Geneva: Skira, 1946); reprinted in Béguin, *Balzac lu et relu* (Paris: Editions du Seuil, 1965).

6. Balzac, *Splendeurs et misères des courtisanes*, Pléiade 6:442; *A Harlot High and Low* (London: Penguin, 1970), 29.

7. *La Cousine Bette* Pléiade 7:377; English trans. Kathleen Raine (New York: Modern Library, 2002), 359.

8. Nineteenth-century thought about sperm is a rich topic, one that has been noted by some scholars: see for instance Harold Aspiz, "Walt Whitman: The Spermatic Imagination," *American Literature* 56:3 (1984): 379–95; Ben Barker-Benfield, "The Spermatic Economy: A Nineteenth-Century View of Sexuality," in *The American Family in Social-Historical Perspective*, ed. Michael Gooden (New York: St. Martin's Press, 1973); see also Rémy de Gourmont, *Physique de l'amour* (Paris: Mercure de France, 1909); English trans. Ezra Pound, *The Natural Philosophy of Love* (New York: Boni & Liveright, 1922).

9. Philarète Chasle, "Introduction," *Contes philosophiques de M. de Balzac* (Paris: Charles Gosselin, 1832), xvi.

10. Peter Brooks, *The Melodramatic Imagination: Balzac, Henry James, Melodrama, and the Mode of Excess* (New Haven: Yale University Press, 1976; reprint, with a new introduction, 1995).

11. J. M. Coetzee, *Disgrace* (London: Martin Secker & Warburg, 1999), 1.

12. When a production of Shakespeare's *Henry VIII* was presented in Paris in 1831, it was under the title *All is True*. Balzac used the phrase as an epigraph to the first edition of *Le Père Goriot*. The story of Goriot and his daughters resembles that of *King Lear*, and in general Balzac was a great admirer of Shakespeare.

13. *Balzac's Lives* (New York: New York Review Books, 2020). The count of the number of characters in *The Human Comedy* comes from Ferdinand Lotte, *Dictionnaire des personnages fictifs de la Comédie Humaine*, reprinted in volume 12 of the Pléiade edition.

INDEX

For the benefit of digital users, indexed terms that span two pages (e.g., 52–53) may, on occasion, appear on only one of those pages.

Accetto, Torquato
  Della dissimulazione onesta 1–2
Adjuda-Pinto, Miguel Marquis d'
  111–14
advertising 51–2
aesthetics 102
Aiglemont, Hélène d' 32–4
Aiglemont, Julie d' 32–4, 47–8
Aiglemont, M. d' 114
Alençon 85–7, 90–1, 97–8
Algeria 78
already read 14–15
ambition 6–8, 20, 52–3, 63–4, 77–9,
  89–90, 97–100, 110–11, 127,
  133–4, 136
Ancien Régime 56–7, 61–2, 65–6, 70,
  85–8, 96–7, 124
Angoulême 61–3, 71
animals 25–6, 28–9, 49, 62–3
appetite 12–13, 21, 23–4, 36, 70, 104–5,
  116, 131, 136
Arabian Nights 20, 118–19
Arcis-sur-Aube 43, 45, 76–80, 111–13
aristocracy/aristocrats 5–6, 16–20,
  34–5, 44–5, 61–2, 77–8, 89–91,
  93–5, 113–14, *see also* nobility/
  nobles
Armande, Mlle 85–9
Army of the Princes 34–5
Arthez, Daniel d' 13–14, 54–5, 107–8
Auerbach, Erich
  Mimesis 84–5
Aurevilly, Barbey d' 67
authority 5–6, 43–4, 55–7, 84–5, 96–8
autobiography 103–4

Bach, Johann Sebastian 1–3
Balzac, Honoré de
  The Abandoned Woman (*La femme
    abandonnée*) 10–11, 47, 113–14
  Analytical Studies (*Études analytiques*)
    98–100
  Another Study of Womankind (*Autre
    étude de femme*) 65–8, 70, 111–13
  Avant-Propos 49, 98–100, 103–4, 110
  Béatrix 32–4
  The Black Sheep (*La Rabouilleuse*)
    19–20, 47
  César Birotteau 114
  The Collection of Antiquities (*Le Cabinet
    des antiques*) 85–6, 135–6
  Cousin Bette (*La cousine Bette*) 19–20,
    32, 120, 125–6, 129–30
  A Daughter of Eve (*Une fille d'Eve*)
    13–14, 114
  The Duchesse de Langeais (*La Duchesse
    de Langeais*) 13–14, 25, 110–11, 119
  Facino Cane 20
  The Fatal Skin (*La Peau de chagrin*)
    10–11, 17–18, 56–7, 73, 120–5, 127
  Ferragus 60–1
  The Girl with the Golden Eyes (*La Fille
    aux yeux d'or*) 25, 30–2, 47, 60–1
  Gobseck 10–12
  A Harlot High and Low (*Splendeurs
    et misères des courtisanes*) 10–12,
    18–19, 34–5, 120–1
  History of the Thirteen (*Histoire des
    Treize*) 60–1
  The House of Nucingen (*La Maison
    Nucingen*) 11–12, 21–4, 96–7

Balzac, Honoré de (*cont.*)
  The Human Comedy (*La Comédie
    humaine*) 3–4, 12–13, 15, 17–20, 24,
    31, 47, 49, 68–70, 73, 78–9, 82–4,
    91–2, 94–101, 110–11, 113–15, 119,
    121–4, 132–6
  The Lily of the Valley (*Le lys dans la
    vallée*) 13–14, 47, 57, 119
  Lost Illusions (*Illusions perdues*) 7, 10–11,
    13–14, 21, 50–7, 71, 78–9, 85–6,
    105–6, 118–19
  Louis Lambert 17–18
  The Marriage Contract (*Le contrat de
    mariage*) 19–20
  Massimila Doni 25
  Melmoth Reconciled (*Melmoth
    réconcilié*) 32–4
  The Member for Arcis (*Le député
    d'Arcis*) 15–16, 45, 76–7, 82–4, 97–8
  Memoirs of Two Young Wives (*Mémoires
    de deux jeunes mariées*) 32–4, 47
  Modeste Mignon 15, 19–20
  A Murky Business (*Une ténébreuse
    affaire*) 15–16, 34–5, 45–6, 75–8,
    97–8, 135–6
  The Old Maid (*La Vieillefille*) 51–2,
    85–6, 135–6
  A Passion in the Desert (*Une passion dans
    le desert*) 25–6, 47, 123–4
  Père Goriot 5–12, 21, 24, 47, 60–3,
    68–9, 78–9, 85–6, 103–4, 111–14, 131
  Philosophical Studies (*Etudes
    philosophiques*) 98–100
  The Provincial Muse (*La Muse du
    département*) 51–3, 71–2
  The Red Inn (*L'Auberge rouge*) 9–10
  Sarrasine 25, 60–1, 69–70, 91–2
  The Search for the Absolute (*La recherche
    de l'Absolu*) 17–18, 98–100, 122–3
  Theory of Movement (*Théorie de la
    démarche*) 98–100
  The Underside of History (*L'Envers de
    l'histoire contemporaine*) 75–6
  The Unknown Masterpiece (*Le chef
    d'oeuvre inconnu*) 122–3
  The Woman of Thirty (*La femme de
    trente ans*) 32–4, 47, 123–4
Balzacian
  ambition 7–8
  concerns 79
    creation 134
    imaginary 120
    method 125–6
    novelist 12–13
    objects 108–9
    prose 136
    young man 123–4
Balzac, Laure 10–11
bankers 5–8, 10–11, 70, 77–8, 92–3, 95–6
bankruptcy 22, 51–2, 93, 95, 118–19
banks 19–22, 87
Bargeton, Louise de 62–3
Barthes, Roland 15, 60–1
battle of
  Dresden 42
  Jena 39–40, 76–7
  Marengo 43–4
  Moskova 42
  Sommo-Sierra 42
Baudraye, Dinah de la 12–13, 51–2, 71–2
Beaupré, Fanny 117
Beauséant, Vicomtesse Claire de 6–8,
  10–11, 47, 92, 111–14
Beauvisage, Cécile 76–9
Beauvisage, Philéas 76–7
Beethoven, Ludwig van 1–2
Béguin, Albert 115–16
Bellegardes 16
Benjamin, Walter 68
  "The Storyteller" 67
Bérénice 105–7, 109–10
Berlioz, Hector 1–2
Bianchon, Horace 13–14, 21, 68–70,
  111–13
Birotteau, César 114–16, 125–6
Birotteau, Césarine 114–15
Birotteau, Constance 114
Bixiou, Jean-Jacques 21–4, 96–7, 117
Blamont-Chauvry, Princesse de 114
Blondet, Emile 13–14, 21–3, 55–6, 58–60
Blücher, General Gebhard von 55
Bois de Vincennes 94–5
Bonaparte, *see* Napoleon
Bonapartists 77–8
Bourbon Restoration 6, 43, 52, 56–7,
  77–8, 82–8, 110–11
Bourbons 36, 39, 43–4, 52, 83–6
bourgeois
  comfort 32–4
  epoch 94

fortune 90–1
issues 129
monarchy 44–5, 88
pharmacist 94–5
progressivism 79–80
solution 127
wives 120–1
women 61–2, 111–13, 120–1
bourgeoisie 65, 76–7, 86–9, 113–14, 127
Brahms, Johannes 2–3
Brazier, Flore 47
Brooks, Peter
    Balzac's Lives 133
    Reading for the Plot 133
    The Melodramatic Imagination 125–6
Brothers of Consolation 17–18
Buloz, François 57
Butor, Michel 12–13

Cadignan, Princesse de,
    see Maufrigneuse
Caen 80–2
Caesar Augustus, Emperor 40, 45–6
Calvin, John 50–1
Calvi, Théodore 18–19
Camusot 105–7
Canalis, Melchior de 15, 19–20
capital 15–16, 22, 54–5, 62, 70, 79, 93–5,
    see also cash, money, wealth
capitalism 93, 95
capitalist 96
    development 133–4
    economy 84–5
    finance 22
    production 73–4
    society 10–11, 97–8
cash 4–5, 78–82, 95–8, 106–7, 120–1,
    see also capital, money, wealth
caste 65, 110–11, 117
    boundaries 85–6
    distinctions 132
    enemy 41–2
Castiglione, Baldassare
    The Courtier 1–2
Catholic women 49
censors/censorship 28–31, 50–3, 56
Chapuys-Montlaville, Baron de 51–3
Chardon 94–5
Chargeboeuf, Marquis de 37–41, 76–7
Chargeboeuf, Vicomte de 76–7

Charles X, King 77–8, 89–90, 93
Château de Cinq-Cygne 36–8, 42, 45,
    76–8
Chateaubriand, François René de 50–1
    René 32
Chaulieu. Louise de 47
Cheat-Death (Trompe-la-Mort) 18–19,
    see also Collin, Herrera, Vautrin
Chesnel, Maître 85–8, 90–1
Chrestien, Michel 107–8
Christie, Agatha 115
Cinq-Cygne family 37–8, 43–4, 46,
    76–80, 82
Cinq-Cygne, Laurence de 35–48, 75–80
Civil Code 89–90
Claës, Balthasar 17–18, 98–100, 122–3
class 65, 76–7, 89–90, 110–11, 131–2
    prejudices 16
    privileges 85–6
Coetzee, J. M.
    Disgrace 127
Coffe 80–2
Collin, Jacques 11–12, 18–20, 95,
    109–10, 114, 116–17, 121–2, see also
    Cheat-Death, Herrera, Vautrin
Comte, Auguste 63–4
Conrad, Joseph 67, 125
Constant, Benjamin 50–1
Convention Nationale 83–4
convicts 8–9, 17–20, 75–6
Coralie 32–4, 58–9, 62–3, 105–10, 115
Corentin 34–8, 43–5, 76–7
Corneille, Pierre
    Cinna 40, 45–6
corruption 50–2, 63–4, 80–2, 87–9,
    92–3, 97–8
Couture 21–2
Crevel, Célestin 125–31
crime/criminals 8–12, 19–20, 87, 92–3,
    95, 103, 125, 129–30
critics/criticism 3–4, 24, 32–4, 53–4,
    58–9, 75–6, 98–100, 115–16, 132–6

Dante 71–2
Dauriat 54–5, 58
Delacroix, Eugène 41–2
Derville, Maître 110–11, 119
desire 7–9, 12–13, 32–5, 48–9, 62–3, 92,
    102, 111–13, 118–26
Dongo, Fabrice del 2

Dostoevsky, Fyodor 96–7
dowry 7–8, 78–9, 90–1, 94–5, 125–6, 128–9
drama 5–6, 11–12, 22, 46, 53–5, 60–1, 73, 77–9, 87, 96–8, 100, 131–3, 135–6, *see also* melodrama
Du Croisier, M. 86–8, 90–1, 97–8
Dudley, Lord 31
Du Val-Noble, Suzanne 117–19

eating and talking 70
egotism 23, 124
Egypt 25–6, 29–30
elections 15–16, 45, 76–84, 89–90, 93, 111–13
Emerson, Ralph Waldo
"Nature" 59–60
Engels, Friedrich 63–4
England 66, 84–5, 100
English 23–4, 66, 100, 131–2
    inventions 66
    lord 31
    novel 132–3, 136
    translations 134–5
    women 62–3, 83–4
Esgrignon, Marquis d' 85–6
Esgrignon, Marquise d' 90–1
Esgrignon, Victurnien d' 12–13, 60–1, 85–91, 97–8, 111–14
Espard, Marquise d' 62–3, 78, 111–13
Euphrasie 32–4

Falstaff 100
Faubourg Saint-Germain 6–7, 44–5, 89, 94–5, 110–11, 113–14
Faulkner, William 85–6, 125
Fendant et Cavalier 54–5
fiction 4–5, 17–18, 51–3, 101, 117–18, 131–3
fictional
    beings 11
    characters 45–6, 133
    economy 10–11
    journalists 29–30, 57
    lives 133
    people/persons 75–6, 110–11, 132–3
    protagonists 41–2
    women 49
    world 12–13, 73–4
finance 11–12, 19–20, 22, 60–1, 79, 92–3, 95, 113–14

Finot, Andoche 21–2
Fischer, Johann 129–30
Fischer, Lisbeth 32, 47, 129–30
Five Swans 35
Florine 107–10, 117
Fontaine, Comte de 115
Fontaine, Comtesse de 115
Fontaine, Emilie 115
Fouché, Joseph 36, 43–5, 75–6
Francesca 71–2
Franchessini, Colonel 10–11, 18–19
Franks 85–6, 90–1
French Empire 40
French Revolution 5–6, 34–5, 38, 41–2, 44–5, 52–3, 56–7, 65–6, 82, 89–90, 125, 133–4
Frenhofer 98–100, 122–3
Freud, Sigmund 73–4, 122–3
furnishings 62–3, 105–11, 114, 118–19, 128
furniture 5–6, 63–4, 103–7, 109–10, 129

Galathionne, Prince 111–13
Galsworthy, John 11
Gauls 85–6, 90–1
German
    accent 70
    businessman 8–9
    diplomat 55
Germany 29–30, 36
Giguet, Colonel 77–8
Giguet, Simon 76–80, 82
Girel of Troyes, Mlle 43
Gobseck 95–6, 119, 121–3
Gobseck, Esther van 48–9, 94–5, 115–18, 120
Gondreville, Malin de 34–5, 37–8, 43–5, 76–9, 82–4
Goriot, Père 5–8, 78–9, 119, 131
Gothard 36
Gothic novel 71–2, 129–30
Goujet, Abbé 36–7
Grandlieu, Clotilde de 94–5, 113–14
Grandlieu, Ducs de 111–13
Grands Fanadels 17–18, 75–6
Granville, Marie-Angélique de 14
Grévin 77–9
Grimm Brothers
    Kinder- und Hausmärchen 68
guillotine 2, 35–7, 42

Hanska, Evelina 63–4
Hauteserre, Adrien d' 34–5, 42–8
Hauteserre brothers 36–8, 42
Hauteserre family 34–7
Hauteserre, Robert d' 34–5, 42
Herder, Johann Gottfried 59–60
Hérouville, Duc d' 120
Herrera, Carlos 18–19, 94–5, 109–10,
    121–2, see also Cheat-Death,
    Collin, Vautrin
high society 65, 91–2, 111–13
Hortense 125–6, 128–30
Hulot, Adeline 120–1, 125–7, 129–31
Hulot d'Ervy, Baron Hector 32, 120,
    125–6

Imperial Eagle 39–49
Indianapolis 3–4
Italy 2, 43–4

Jacobins 34–5, 83–4
James, Henry 4–5, 17–20, 67, 75–6,
    97–8, 125, 132–6
    The American 16–17
    The Golden Bowl 3–4
    "The Lesson of Balzac" 3–4
journalism/journalists 13–14, 21, 50–60,
    62–3, 67, 71–3, 97–8, 107–10,
    118–19, 121–2
July Monarchy 79–82
July Revolution 44–5, 52, 56–7, 82,
    84–6, 88, 90–1, 93–5, 111–13

Karamazov, Ivan 96–7
Keller bank 87
Keller, Charles 78–9
Keller, François 77–8, 82
Kipling, Rudyard 67

Lacan, Jacques 7–8
Laclos, Pierre Choderlos de
    Les Liaisons dangereuses 1–2
Lafayette, Madame de 1–2
Lamartine, Alphonse de 15
Lambert, Louis 17–18, 98–100, 121–3
Langeais, Antoinette de 48–9,
    110–13, 119
Langeais, Duchesse de 17–18
Lanty family 60–1
Lanty, Mme de 91–2

La Rochefoucauld, François de 1–2
Lefebvre, Robert 44–5
Légion d'Honneur 28–9, 93, 125–6
legitimacy 57, 79–80, 84–5, 100
Legitimist
    high society 111–13
    nobles/nobility 80–2, 85–6
    principles 44–5
    votes 78–9
Legitimists 79–80
Lenoncourt, Duc de 114
Leskov, Nikolai 67–8
Leuwen, Lucien 2, 80–2
liberals 77–8, 86–7
Lorrain, Pierrette 119
Louis XVI, King 83–4
Louis XVIII, King 77–8, 83–4, 89–90
Louis-Philippe, King 44–5, 66, 77–80,
    82–4
LousteauÉtienne 51–2, 56–60, 71–2,
    107–10, 115–17
love/lovers 2–3, 5–11, 13–16, 19–20, 23–5,
    27, 29–36, 44–5, 48–9, 51–2, 60–3,
    68–72, 78–9, 87, 94–5, 97–8,
    105–14, 116–17, 119, 121–3, 127,
    129–30, 132–4
Lukács, Georg 50–1, 84–5, 97–8
Luther, Martin 50–1

Mairobert, M. 80–2
Malvaut, Fanny 119
Manerville, Natalie de 14
manners 1–2, 23, 84–5, 98–100, 115–16
Marneffe, Valérie 32, 47, 120, 129–31
marriage 5–9, 13–14, 21, 32–5, 42–9,
    62–4, 78–9, 83–4, 86–95, 98–100,
    113–14, 125–30
Marsay, Henri de 8–9, 13–14, 30–2,
    44–5, 68–9, 83–4, 87, 111–14
Martin, M. 25–6
Marx, Karl 63–4
    The Communist Manifesto 93
Massiac, Eugène de 10–11
Maufrigneuse, Diane de (Princesse de
    Cadignan) 13–14, 44–5, 87–91,
    111–14
Maufrigneuse, Georges de 44–5
Maupassant, Guy de 67
Maupin, Camille, see Touches
melodrama 2–4, 17, 73, 125–32, 134–6

Michu 34–8, 40–5, 77–8
Michu, François 76–7
Michu, Marthe 36–8
Mignon, Modeste 19–20
Mignonne (panther) 26–30, 47, 123–4
Mirah, Josépha 120, 125–9
Mirouët, Ursule 117, 119
modernism 134–5
modernity 2–5, 34–5, 59–60, 96–7, 102, 133–4
money 5–6, 8–11, 19–21, 23–4, 32, 58–65, 80–4, 87, 89–98, 105–7, 109–10, 119–24, 128, see also capital, cash, wealth
Montriveau, General Armand de 13–14, 17–18, 68–9, 111–14
Mortsauf, Henriette de 13–14, 32–4, 47–9, 119, 123–4
Mozart, Wolfgang Amadeus 1–2

Napoleon 6, 25–6, 34–46, 52–3, 55, 68–9, 75–7, 79–80, 82–4, 86–7, 89–90
Napoleonic
  creed 86–7
  epic 133–4
  France 4–5
  past 77–8
  regime 34–5
  wars 82
Nathan, Raoul 13–14, 56–9, 117
National Assembly 50–2, 83–4, 89–90, 93
Newman, Christopher 16
newspapers 50–8, 106–7
  Journal des Débats 51–2
  La Presse 51–2
  Le Messager 51–2
  Le Réveil 118–19
nobility/nobles 23, 34–7, 39, 42, 61–2, 65, 68–9, 76–7, 80–2, 85–92, 110–11, see also aristocracy/aristocrats
Nodesme forest 36–7
Normandy 80–2, 111–13
Norman servant 32
Norman town 85–6
Notre-Dame Cathedral 39
Nucingen, Augusta de 83–4
Nucingen, Baron de 7–8, 10–14, 22, 59–60, 70, 83–4, 93–6, 116–18

Nucingen, Delphine de 7–11, 13–14, 19–20, 23–4, 68–9, 97–8, 119

Olympia, or Roman Vengeance (Olympia, ou les vengeances romaines) 71–2

Palais-Royal 54–5, 123–4
Paolo 71–2
Paquita 30–1, 47
Paris 5–8, 17–18, 25–6, 30–2, 36–7, 44–5, 52–5, 61–4, 71–2, 78, 83–7, 91–2, 94–8, 114, 116, 121–2, 128
Parisian
  crowd 60–1
  dandies 22
  fashion 62–3
  journalism 109–10
  journalist 51–2
  life 18–19, 103–4
  love 119
  manifestation 7
  restaurant 21
  social networks 18–19
  society 78–9, 111–13
Parlement de Paris 50–1
passion 14, 25–34, 40, 106–7, 111–13, 116, 120–2
paternal authority 5–6, 96–7
Pension Vauquer 5–6, 8–9, 13–14, 22–3, 60–1, 103–5, 111–14, 133
Père-Lachaise cemetery 23, 106–7
Peyrade 34–8, 76–7
Philadelphia 3–4
physiognomy 60–1
Piketty, Thomas 92
  Capital in the Twenty-first Century 79
Pius VII, Pope 39
Plato 70
police 11–12, 18–19, 34–8, 43–4, 62, 95
politics 2–3, 13–16, 34–5, 44–5, 50–2, 55–7, 63–4, 76–85, 116, 124
Portenduère, Madame de 68–9
poverty 8–9, 54–5, 104–5, 108–10, 116, 120
power 1–3, 15–24, 32–4, 36, 57, 59–60, 77–9, 83–4, 90–1, 124
prostitutes/courtisanes 32–4, 47–51, 54–5, 94–5, 109–11, 115–23
Protestant women 49
Proust, Marcel 25, 32
  In Search of Lost Time 97–8

Prussia 39
Prussians 41, 55

Rastignac, Eugène de 5–14, 18–24, 60–3, 78–9, 83–4, 87, 92–3, 96–8, 111–14, 117, 119
Reign of Terror 34–5
Renaissance 70
representation 32, 59–60, 73, 76–7, 84–5, 98–100, 103–4, 106–7, 109–10, 115–16, 125–6, 129–30, 134–6
Restaud, Anastasie de 6–7, 10–12, 78–9, 111–13
Restaud, Comtesse de 6–7
Rochefide, Berthe de 113–14
Rochefide, Marquise de 69–70, 91–2
Ronquerolles, Marquis de 111–14
Rosanvallon, Pierre 63–4
Rousseau, Jean-Jacques 2, 102–3
    The New Héloise 102
    Confessions 102
    Emile 50–1
    The Social Contract 50–1
Rubempré, Lucien Chardon de 12–14, 18–20, 32–4, 48–55, 57–63, 65–6, 71–2, 78, 92, 94–8, 105–17, 121–2
Russia 17–18, 29–30
Russian 111–13
    campaign 68–9
    periodical 57
    prince 65

Sade, Marquis de
    One Hundred Twenty Days of Sodom 103
Saint Louis 3–4
Sainte-Beuve, Charles Augustin 32–4
    "On Industrial Literature" 53–4
Saki (H. H. Monroe) 67
San Francisco 3–4
Sancerre 71–2
Sand, George 51–2
San-Réal, Marquise de 30–1
Sarrasine 60–1
Sartre, Jean-Paul
    La Nausée 41–2
Scheherazade 118–19
Scotland 84–5
Scott, Walter 5–6, 49, 54–5, 84–5, 132

seduction/seductive 52–3, 65, 71–2, 86–9, 106–7, 126–7, 132
serial novel (*roman-feuilleton*) 51–4
Sérisy, Vicomte de 111–14
sex/sexuality 1–2, 7–9, 18–19, 25, 28–34, 36, 47–9, 60–1, 106–7, 116–19, 122–4, 127–8
Shakespeare, William 133
    Henry IV Part 1 100
    Henry IV Part 2 100
    Henry V 100
    Richard II 100
Siegfried 32
Sieglinde 32
Siegmund 32
Sieyès, Emmanuel 75–6
signs 60–6, 73–4, 133–4
Simeuse, Marie-Paul 34–8, 42, 76–80
Simeuse, Paul-Marie 34–8, 42, 76–80
Sorel, Julien 2
Spain 19–20, 29–31
Spanish nobleman 68–9
Spanish priest 10–11, 18–19, 95, 109–10
Stendhal 1–4, 6, 52–3, 84–5
    The Charterhouse of Parma 82
    Lucien Leuwen 2–3, 80–2
    The Red and the Black 82
storytelling 67–8, 70–1, 73–4, 118–19
Sue, Eugène
    The Mysteries of Paris (Les mystères de Paris) 51–2

Tacitus 50–1
Taillefer, Jean-Frédéric 8–10, 92–3
Taillefer, Michel-Frédéric 8–11
Taillefer, Victorine 8–10, 23–4, 92–3
Taine, Hippolyte 92
Talleyrand, Charles-Maurice de 39–40, 75–6
The Thirteen 17–18, 75–6, 78–9, 83–4, 111–13
Thierry, Augustin 90–1
to say everything 47–8, 82, 102–4, 110–11
Touches, Félicité des (Camille Maupin) 13–14, 66, 71, 111–14
Trailles, Maxime de 78–9, 83–4, 87, 111–13
Troyes 34–5, 37–8, 42–3, 83–4
Tuileries 61–3, 92

United Kingdom 134–5
United States 3–4, 85–6, 134–5
Uxelles, Marquise d' 114

Valentin, Raphaël de 12–13, 17–18, 56–7, 60–1, 120–4
Valéry, Paul 34–5
Vandenesse, Félix de 13–14, 32–4, 48–9, 114, 121–2
Vauquer, Madame 103–4
Vautrin 8–12, 18–20, 23–4, 32, 92–7, 109–10, 114, 121–2, *see also* Cheat-Death, Collin, Herrera
vengeance 14, 30–2, 68–72, 125–6, 129–30
Verdi, Giuseppe 2–3

vice 5–6, 61–2, 78–9, 108–10, 120, 131
Vignon, Claude 55–6
virtue 23, 47–9, 96–7, 109–10, 119–20, 131
Voltaire 2, 50–1

Wagner, Richard 2–3
  Die Walküre 32
Wars of Religion 54–5
wealth 59–61, 89–92, 96, 118–19, 125–6, *see also* capital, cash, money
Wilde, Oscar 4–5, 96–7

Zambinella 60–1, 69–70, 91–2
Zola, Emile 11
  Pot-Bouille 111–13